Infected Christianity
A Study of Modern Racism

Infected Christianity

A Study of Modern Racism

ALAN DAVIES

McGill-Queen's University Press
Kingston and Montreal

© McGill-Queen's University Press 1988
ISBN 0-7735-0651-9

Legal deposit 2nd quarter 1988
Bibliothèque nationale du Québec

∞

Printed in Canada on acid-free paper   ·

This book has been published with the help of a grant from the Canadian Federation for the Humanities, using funds provided by the Social Sciences and Humanities Research Council of Canada.

Canadian Cataloguing in Publication Data

Davies, Alan T.
    Infected Christianity   ·
    Includes bibliographical references and index.
    ISBN 0-7735-0651-9
    1. Racism–Religious aspects–Christianity.
    2. Race relations–Religious aspects–Christianity.
    I. Title.
    BT734.2.D38 1988   261.8'348   C88-09009-1

To Marilyn, Drew, and Alison

Contents

Preface

The phrase "Infected Christianity" is taken from a chapter subtitle in George L. Mosse's recent history of European racism, *Toward the Final Solution*. Mosse writes:

Racism had sought an alliance with the main trends of the [nineteenth] century: nationalism, spiritualism, bourgeois morality, and the belief in science. But it also reached out to Christianity, in spite of its own claim to a monopoly over salvation ... There were many pious Christians and good churchmen who consistently rejected racism, and others, such as the Quakers, who equally consistently helped the oppressed. But the record of most Protestant churches and of the Catholic Church was not one clearly opposed to the idea of racism.[1]

This book is an attempt to elucidate this theme in a more detailed fashion. Consequently, I have isolated and examined five modern "Christs" as examples of the racist contamination of Christianity since the rise of racism as a secular ideology in the West. I have also considered the moral and spiritual implications of these new christologies. Since Germany has played a pivotal role in recent history in many respects, but in this respect especially, I have placed the Germanic Christ first in my series and have written most extensively about the racist contamination of German Christianity. Indeed, as the reader will soon discover, the shadow of the German philosopher Johann-Gottlieb Fichte falls over more than the future course of German nationalism and German racism alone. France, I believe is second in importance, both because race doctrines were invented largely on French soil, and because of the internal conflicts of the Third Republic which assisted the rise of fascism; hence, the Latin Christ follows. Since the age of racism was also the age of imperialism, and the Anglo-Saxons (including the Anglo-Americans) were the most successful imperialists of the modern world, as well as the most enthusiastic proponents of Social Darwinism, the Anglo-Saxon Christ is the third racial Christ to be examined. South Africa, that troubled white republic, has replaced Nazi Germany as the paradigmatic racist state of the twentieth century; the Afrikaner Christ, therefore, comes fourth. Finally, as the result of a resurgence of black nationalism in America, I have scrutinized the black Christ advocated by some current black theologians and churchmen.

Racism, as the term is employed in these pages, is a worldview, variously defended on biological, cultural, historical, and even religious grounds, in which the idea of race is placed at the centre of human concerns as a first principle. This, of course, is a general definition, which can be refined to distinguish between the different methods of realizing racist values and their more or less virulent expressions. As Marcus Singer has pointed out, a degree of confusion and even contradiction has bedevilled contemporary discussion of racism (or racialism), especially regarding the validity of the use of the word "race."[2] Well-known authorities such as Ashley Montagu[3] and Ruth Benedict[4] are not always clear or precise in their characterizations, at least not when nuances and shades of meaning are examined. Paradoxically, while racism presupposes the division of the human species into discrete entities called races, the racist phenomenon, or "racemania," to cite Singer again, transcends the racial reality.[5] It has a fictional quality and no more relies on the existence of real races than antisemitism relies on the existence of real Jews; the racist authors of the nineteenth century more or less invented their own races and spun their theories accordingly. Racially homogeneous societies can be suffused with the racist worldview, and racially heterogeneous societies can be devoid of its destabilizing presence. This does not mean that the rise of racial speculation in European civilization did not supply the foundations for the rise of modern racism; as we shall see, it did. But, as we shall also see, the study of race and racism are by no means the same. The latter, rather than the former, is my subject.

As a Christian, I regard racism as fundamentally incompatible with Christianity: "He created every race of men of one stock, to inhabit the whole earth's surface" (Acts 17:26). Unfortunately, however, other Christians have not always concurred. Why? Why have both Catholics and Protestants allowed themselves to become infected with the racist disease? What elements in Lutheranism, for example, rendered the Lutheran tradition vulnerable, thereby contributing to the reception of racist ideas in the birthplace of the Protestant Reformation? What elements in Dutch Calvinism had a similar effect in South African history? Why did French Catholicism succumb during the period of the Third Republic? What made the social gospel movement in American Protestantism susceptible? Why is black American Protestantism today also susceptible?

I have attempted to answer these questions, although I do not claim to have explored every aspect. Nor do I claim to have investigated the other side of the matter, i.e., the Christian struggle *against* racism, with the exception of occasional references to men such as Bartolomé de Las Casas, Alonso de Cartegena, and Dietrich Bonhoeffer. If a distorted portrait is to be avoided, this omission must be acknowledged. After all, the "pious Christians and good churchmen" who fought against racist ideas are also part of the Christian legacy. In the past, their efforts were frequently futile, not merely because their numbers were relatively small, but because of other factors as well, notably the "individualistic illusions" to which Protestants especially are prone,[6] causing them to underestimate the depth of the problem. Despite these illusions, however, the Quakers (whom Mosse praises), inspired by their doctrine of the inner light, recognized the essential humanity of the black Africans and strongly objected to the institution of slavery;[7] so did John Wesley, the father of Methodism, in one of the greatest of his tracts.[8] Even in late nineteenth-century France, when the Aryan myth was fastening its lethal grip on the Catholic imagination and racist feelings (mostly against Jews) were rampant in clerical circles, the voice of Catholic protest against the new ideology made itself heard: "The blood that flowed on Calvary for the redemption of mankind, the blood that our old painters picture to us caught up in chalices and golden bowls by the hands of angels, was Jewish blood, Semitic blood. Neither Mary, mother of Jesus, nor John, his well-beloved disciple, nor Simon, called Cephas, nor any of the Twelve Apostles, was of Aryan descent."[9] And, in our day, we have the heroic example of Christians such as the ex-Afrikaner Nationalist Beyers Naudé. When reading the following chapters with Mosse's negative judgment in mind, it is important to remember these counter-testimonies.

This book is a study in the history of ideas. Stating this immediately raises a question: do ideas affect the ebb and flow of historical currents as the revolutions of the moon affect the ocean tides, or are they merely epiphenomena – surface manifestations in the realm of consciousness of subterranean forces that constitute the real arbiters of history? If the latter position is adopted, a work such as the following must be regarded as essentially erroneous, the product of a false "idealism" that attaches too much significance to ideas as ideas, while ignoring the more important non-ideational aspects of reality. If this view is accepted, there is no compelling reason to link anti-semitism, for example, to the holocaust, or racism to apartheid, at least in a simple cause-and-effect fashion; presumably, these racist explosions can be more adequately explained by economic, political, and social causes on the material level of our historical existence. I do not deny that non-ideational factors are involved in racism; *ressentiment*, for example (a feeling, not an idea) is clearly one such factor and in the course of my analysis I draw attention both to its presence and to its social roots. However, I believe that ideas impinge in a serious and significant fashion on the stuff of history and play a decisive role in human affairs. Ideas, in my opinion, are not merely epiphenomena; they also shape the world for good or ill. Consequently, while neither the holocaust nor apartheid can be explained exclusively by the history of ideas, they cannot be explained apart from this history. Christianity, moreover, is implicated in both the ideological and material facets of the human story: it is implicated ideologically through its dogmas and materially through its power. In this investigation, however, the focus is on the former.

No author is an island, and it only remains for me to thank my friends and colleagues who have helped me along the way. I am grateful to Terry Anderson, Gregory Baum, Jim Gollnick, Paul Perron, Jack Robson, Hans Rollmann, and Polly Winsor for their advice and encouragement at different stages in the slow evolution of this work. Needless to say, however, I alone am responsible for any errors it may contain. In addition, I wish to record my gratitude to the secretarial staff of Victoria College, notably June Hewitt and Jackie Ong, and to Karen Levitt, who prepared the index, Rea Wilmshurst, who typed and corrected the final draft, as well as to the editors of McGill-Queen's University Press. A generous Leave Fellowship from the Social Sciences and Humanities Research Council of Canada enabled me to finish what I had begun erstwhile, but might never have completed otherwise.

Material in chapter one has been adapted from: "The Aryan Myth: A Motif in Christian Anti-Semitism," *Journal of Ecumenical Studies*; "The Aryan Myth: Its Religious Significance," *Studies in Religion*; and "Racism and German Protestant Theology: A Prelude to the Holocaust," *The Annals of the American Academy of Political and Social Science*.

Infected Christianity

CHAPTER ONE

From Racial Ethnocentrism to Racism: Some Historical Reflections

Although racism itself is a fairly recent phenomenon in Western history, its roots are ancient and varied. Its basic root, however, is ethnocentrism, a modern term which means the universal instinct to identify humankind with the members of one's own tribe, community, or nation, and to regard outsiders as less than fully human, although this designation need not be explicit.[1] So deeply embedded in human nature is the ethnocentric impulse that among preliterate peoples tribal names are invariably synonyms for "humans" or "humanity."[2] Even with the dawn of civilization and the advent of a more sophisticated awareness, ethnocentrism failed to disappear; instead, it appeared in a sublimated form with pretensions unknown to more simple societies, and posed a much more serious problem. *Racial* ethnocentrism is the play of racial images (colour, physical type, intelligence, etc.) in attitudes of cultural and social superiority adopted by one group or collectivity toward other groups and collectivities. These images can be clearly or vaguely defined. Colour consciousness, for example, arose slowly and sporadically in the history of the West; consequently, it is inaccurate to regard racial notions as having existed in the same measure from the beginning. We are not dealing with constants, but with a series of accretions.

ANCIENT ETHNOCENTRISM

Ethnocentrism was present everywhere among ancient peoples, in India and China as well as in Greece and Rome. Classical civilization, despite its Stoic (i.e., cosmopolitan) components, always retained as its ineradicable basis an underlying sense of Greek superiority. While the term "race" (*genos, ethnos, gens*), when employed by ancient writers, bore none of its modern racialistic connotations (although some modern historians, themselves tainted with antisemitism, sought to convey this impression of attitudes toward Jews in antiquity),[3] there is ample evidence of Greco-Roman condescension toward alien, less "civilized" peoples. Aristotle, in particular, considered all non-Hellenes innately inferior, arguing that barbarians, since they lacked reason, were subordinate to the Greeks as the body was subordinate to the soul. "Wherefore Hellenes do not like to call Hellenes slaves, but confine the term to barbarians. Yet, in using this language, they really mean the natural slave of whom we spoke at first; for it must be admitted that some are slaves everywhere, others nowhere."[4] Aristotle was no doubt influenced by Plato, for whom Greeks and barbarians were natural foes and between whom warfare was a natural state of affairs, as between certain species of animals, birds, and reptiles.[5]

Greek ethnocentrism crumbled to some extent when Aristotle's illustrious pupil Alexander the Great conquered the Persians and discovered that his new subjects were not by nature his mentor's barbarian slaves, but members of a different, highly developed culture. As a result, "the practical demands of imperial statescraft ... persuaded Alexander to abandon ... the parochialism of his distinguished tutor and to adopt some of the teachings of the Stoic philosopher Zeno" in order to construct a new and "wider *homonoia* than hitherto had been envisaged."[6] Nevertheless, the parochial feeling of Greek superiority lingered at the core of even the universal society that Alexander sought to establish, so that the Hellenistic Greek could still think of himself as the privileged bearer of enlightenment to the subject peoples in terms only slightly less narrow than Aristotle's. When the later Seleucid king Antiochus IV Epiphanes placed a statue of the pagan god Zeus in the Holy of Holies of the temple in Jerusalem (167 B.C.E.), his intention was to emancipate the benighted Jews from their tribal barbarism by granting them the benefits of Greek religion. This proud and condescending religious and cultural ethnocentrism seems to have been the main source of whatever anti-Jewish sentiments existed in the ancient world.[7] Its extent, however, is uncertain; the Jews were also admired by the Greeks and Romans.[8]

But the ethnocentric pride of the classical epoch was never really a *racial* pride, and even Aristotle with his parochial vision and his natural slaves can scarcely be described as a racist as the term is used today. He is more accurately seen as an insular Greek whose insularity is uncritically revealed in his political reflections. Greco-Roman society, as Frank M. Snowden shows, while fully aware of colour and other physical differences between human beings, was

singularly devoid of racial prejudice. "The Greeks and Romans attached no special stigma to colour, regarding yellow hair or blue
eyes a mere geographical accident, and developed no special racial
theory about the inferiority of darker peoples qua darker peoples."[9]
There was even a tendency in classical letters to idealize the black
Ethiopian as pious and just.[10] When ancient artists placed white and
black figures in juxtaposition on vases and other works of art, they
did so for aesthetic rather than racial reasons, with a pleasant and
harmonious visual contrast in mind.[11] The goddess Isis, whose cult
flourished in the Roman empire, had black priests,[12] and, initially
at least, the newer religion of Christianity adopted the accepting
attitude toward racially different types of humanity of its Greco-
Roman milieu. Did not the Song of Songs celebrate the beauty of
the black Shulamite who stirred the king's love, and did not Paul,
perhaps inspired by the poet Menander, emphasize the oneness of
every kind of person in Christ?[13] Moreover, in his commentary on
the Song of Songs, the Alexandrine exegete Origen staunchly defended
the black woman against the haughty daughters of Jerusalem who
despised her lack of descent from Abraham, Isaac, and Jacob. They
should not have forgotten the leprosy God inflicted on Mary (Miriam)
for having criticized Moses for his marriage to a black Cushite woman
(Numbers 12).[14]

However, as Marvin Pope points out, Origen's apparent approval
of negritude in the name of the universal gospel was ambivalent.[15]
The woman, an allegory for the gentile church, was black by virtue
of her sins and beautiful by virtue of her repentance. When the black
but beautiful soul "rises to greater things and begins to climb from
the lowly to the lofty," she will be made white.[16] Black and white,
in other words, were not only colour-designating terms in ancient
Christian usage, but also vivid and potent metaphors with opposite
religious and moral connotations. To the Hebrews, white symbolized
purity and innocence – "hence it was the dress of the high priest
on the Day of Atonement, and the angels, as holy, appear in white
clothing" – while black, which "absorbs all colours and thus buries
the light" symbolized "death, humiliation, mourning."[17] These associations were certainly older than Hebrew religion, perhaps as old
as time itself, since the interplay between light and life and darkness
and death is part of nature and easily derived from the most basic
elements in human experience. "Whiteness brings to mind the light,
ascension into the bright realm, the immaculateness of virgin snow
… and the transparency of limpid air …"[18] Origen, therefore, was
not affirming the black woman in her blackness as such; rather,
having identified lucidity and reason as well as innocence and purity

with light,[19] he was urging the black soul to become white in order to taste of heavenly bliss.

As Snowden demonstrates, this metaphorical dualism became a general pattern in the writings of the church fathers. "For Christian writers of the first centuries after Christ, it made no difference whether one was as racially different as the Scythian or the Ethiopian ... they regarded as black all men who had not been illuminated by God's light and considered all men, regardless of the color of their skin, as potentially Christians."[20] Because, for the neo-Platonic theologians, the soul rather than the body was the object of redemption, the flesh was not important, and therefore its colour was not important. While this is certainly true, so is its deeper implication: Christ came into the world to make blacks "radiantly bright," i.e., to make them inwardly if not outwardly *white*.[21]

Skin colour, however, was regarded as important in at least part of the ancient world, for the notion that blackness can be the result of a curse also had early origins. First suggested in rabbinic literature,[22] it seeped into Christianity as well, although at a later period.[23] The text on which this claim was based – the curse pronounced by Noah on his grandson Canaan, the son of Ham, because Ham had gazed on his father's nakedness when Noah was in a drunken stupor – was ripe for eventual racial exploitation. During the modern slave era, as we shall see, it played a crucial role in rendering black slavery congenial to Christian morality.

> Cursed be Canaan;
> a slave of slaves shall he be to his brothers ...
> Blessed by the LORD my God be Shem;
> and let Canaan be his slave.
> God enlarge Japheth,
> and let him dwell in the tents of Shem;
> and let Canaan be his slave.   (Genesis 9:25–7)

Ham, according to the rabbis, was "smitten in his skin," i.e., blackened.[24] No doubt the proximity of the Near East to Africa prompted this racial exegesis, which is certainly not supported by the text itself. Interestingly, the earliest anti-black discriminatory measure in recorded history was an inscription on a pillar raised by the pharaoh Sesostris III at the second cataract of the Nile about two millennia before the birth of Jesus.[25] (On the other hand, during the reigns of darker-skinned pharaohs from southern Egypt, anti-white feelings were not unknown.)[26] Snowden recognizes among "certain circles" in antiquity the presence of more "ominous" feelings toward

Ethiopians because of the affinity between blackness and "death, the underworld and evil."[27] Ancient society, consequently, was not entirely colour-blind, and early Christianity, despite its supposed universalism, was undoubtedly infected by these feelings. Christian asceticism, particularly in Egypt, soon intensified the association of darkness with evil by attaching demonic and bestial qualities to the skin colour of Africans, as certain edifying tales from the Egyptian desert fathers of the early church illustrate. In one such tale, the spirit of sexual lust, the devil's snare, is personified as a negro:[28] an image obviously conjured up by the nearby black world. Although race consciousness developed slowly in western culture, its germination was early.

Not only Christian asceticism but Christian theology became infected. Since light is white, the divine *Logos* itself, incarnate in the Christ, must also be white or else it could not conquer the darkness that engulfs both the world and the soul in its redemptive mission. Even prior to Christ – at the moment of creation – the *Logos* was white: the metaphysical antithesis between light and darkness was used to "symbolize being and existence, on the one hand, and non-being or chaos, on the other."[29] White and black, therefore, were elevated to the status of ontological as well as moral designations, and the character of all subsequent Christian thought was firmly set in this intellectual mould. As long as Christian theology was written by white theologians, that is to say, virtually until the present day, this pattern was not seen as tainted with racial assumptions. Such a charge would have seemed absurd to every generation except the current one, and still seems absurd to conservative defenders of the classical tradition. Nevertheless, this ontological dualism constitutes a serious problem for non-white Christians, especially for black theologians, at least one of whom has wondered publicly (and facetiously) if God is a "white racist."[30]

MEDIEVAL AND POST-MEDIEVAL CHRISTENDOM

When classical civilization finally expired, it bequeathed to its medieval Christian successor these ominous racial associations as an enduring legacy. That Satan, the ruler of the underworld, was frequently portrayed as black and bestial in Christian art and literature was one of their fruits. For "blackness suggests the infernal streams of the bowels of the earth, the pit of hell, the devil's color."[31] Examples of this connection are plentiful. A thirteenth-century miracle story from a Cistercian abbey in the Rhineland, in which the devil visits a sceptical knight, informs its readers that the father of evil is "like a gigantic man, very huge and very *black*" (italics mine).[32] Similarly, when Jews (and official clergy) were demonized by heretical sectarians during the more violent spasms in the religious conflicts of the Middle Ages, they were frequently lumped together as a "foul black host" in contrast to the "clean white army of the Saints."[33] Naturally, the foul black host had to be wiped off the face of the earth. Such images were abundant in folkloric and popular conceptions of witches, demons, and the like. Africans themselves were sometimes included with the "monstrous races" clustered at the edge of the world, both geographically and symbolically removed as far as possible from Christ.[34] The Europeans, of course, placed themselves as close as possible.

Indeed, to the medieval Christian imagination it was entirely appropriate to conceive of a white Christian realm (Europe) encircled by menacing pagan realms that were both literally and figuratively darker: a world in which the "children of light" were surrounded by the "children of darkness." "Surrounded" is not strictly accurate, since the western sea was commonly regarded as the edge of the world (at least until Columbus), and Jerusalem rather than Rome was considered the real centre of Christendom and, indeed, of the universe itself.[35] This was perhaps the most ethnocentric notion of all. It was Greco-Roman *hauteur* in a new religious key: Christendom saw itself as the heir of Rome as well as its restoration, and this conviction led both to crusades against the children of darkness, and, in due course, to colonial expansion as a kind of final crusade.[36] At the least, colonialism represented a tremendous outburst of the European "cultural, racial, political and social 'superiority-complex,'"[37] whose effects are still evident today.

Given this general scheme of things, it is not surprising that colour contrast as a code for the most trenchant moral and spiritual dualism became firmly implanted in the Western psyche. Literature, especially during the Renaissance, abounds in famous instances. William Shakespeare, as every student knows, invented a mythical black (Othello) as well as a mythical Jew (Shylock). Othello is the "lusty Moor" whose blackness and burning desire are riveted together by a double connotation involving the "sexuality of beasts and the bestiality of sex."[38] In Elizabethan times, Winthrop Jordan remarks, white and black signified "purity and filthiness, virginity and sin, virtue and baseness, beauty and ugliness, beneficence and evil, God and the devil."[39]

Like their Greco-Roman predecessors, whose cultural pride they imitated so closely, the Europeans became increasingly tainted by quite definite racial ideas stemming largely from their Christian religious formation. Both Catholic and Protestant Christians (especially Calvinists), as Roger Bastide has demonstrated, wove these ideas into their social mores as they settled in new colonies on alien shores: the children of light transplanted into the midst of the children of darkness, or, in neo-Calvinist terms, the elect whites dwelling amid the reprobate blacks.[40] Thus Christianity encouraged self-righteous convictions, and Christian theology, through its colour code, contributed indirectly to the rise of racist ideology in the nineteenth century. While racism proper is a modern phenomenon, racial thought preceded the rise of racism by approximately four hundred years. When the final crusade of colonialism was launched in the fifteenth century, and Europeans began to encounter unprecedented numbers of unfamiliar peoples in remote corners of the earth, speculation concerning the nature of rce was stimulated enormously. Not surprisingly, new questions were raised. The conquest of the Americas soon encouraged thoughts of slavery in relation to the indigenous Americans, misnamed "Indians." White Christians could not be enslaved, of course, but what of the coloured races whose place was clearly much lower on nature's scale? Were the native Americans "natural slaves" in the Aristotelian sense who therefore could be enslaved in good conscience, or did they possess rational souls, making them suitable candidates for baptism rather than slavery? Pope Paul III, in a remarkable apostolic letter (1537), answered the question by proclaiming the so-called Indians to be "true men" fully capable of conversion and entitled to "liberty and dominion" as well as to humane treatment at white hands; under no circumstances should they be reduced to the inhumanity of slavery.[41]

The same issue was debated only a few years later (1550–1) in Valladolid, Spain, by the missionary bishop Bartolomé de Las Casas and the humanist scholar Juan Ginés de Sepúlveda. The bishop vigorously protested against the "natural slave" designation for native Americans, a stance that demonstrated not merely his personal integrity but also the capacity of Christian universalism, when uncorrupted by egotism and spiritual blindness, to transcend even religiously sanctified ethnocentrism. "Surely God," he predicted in 1564, "will wreak his fury and anger against Spain some day for the unjust wars waged against the American Indians."[42] Las Casas, however, was an unusual figure who sought to swim against an extremely powerful tide. Although he accomplished some reforms, the widespread belief in racial superiority, in conjunction with economic self-interest, was simply too strong to be overcome by theological arguments, even with papal and royal support.

Late medieval Spain was also the site of another noteworthy debate with profound theological and social implications. This debate had nothing to do with Aristotle, the discovery of the Americas, or the inauguration of slavery, but, more than any of these, anticipated racist developments in the late nineteenth and early twentieth centuries. Not surprisingly, Christians in the Iberian peninsula, which had been reclaimed for Christianity by the sword and was poised above the lost Christian territories of North Africa, developed, partly for political reasons, an obsession with religious unity. This zeal soon inspired the persecution and forced conversion of religious minorities (Jews and Muslims), with expulsion as the final option for those who refused to convert. Many Spanish Jews accepted baptism, bringing into the church a tide of "New Christians" (*Conversos*) who were eligible for prestigious offices in the ecclesiastical and social hierarchy. The "Old Christians," often less well educated and less wealthy than the New Christians, resented these unwelcome rivals in their midst; the latter, in their eyes, remained aliens in spite of their baptism. Since, however, they *had* been baptized, the former theological arguments for oppressing Jews in Christian society were no longer applicable and a new rationale for discrimination had to be invented. This led to the ingenious concept of "purity of blood" (*limpieza de sangre*): the notion that pure Spanish descent was a necessary prerequisite for office in the church – Jewish and Moorish descent did not qualify.[43] Baptism, the sacrament that washed away sin, evidently could not wash away the taint of race.

Beginning in Toledo in 1449, the highly important religious orders began to legislate against the *Conversos* on racial grounds. This was the first such legislation in Western history, and, as various commentators have noted, a striking prelude and analogue to the Aryan laws of the German Third Reich.[44] As Albert Sicroff points out, the Spanish Catholics rediscovered the Jew concealed within the convert, and this rediscovery released the anti-Jewish passions of the Christian ages in a different guise.[45] Hatred was transposed from a religious into a racial key; a step fraught with peril for those whose blood was regarded as impure, since it left no escape. The full implications of this development, however, had to await the rise of secularism and the politics of the twentieth century.

Remarkably, the late medieval pope Nicholas IV stoutly repudiated the heretical new statutes in a papal bull, but was unable to annul them successfully.[46] This drift into racial legislation in fifteenth- and sixteenth-century Spain also prompted an internal argument in the Spanish church concerning the nature of human unity; it is both noteworthy and prophetic that some Catholic theologians of the day, especially Alonso Diaz de Montalvo and Alonso de Cartegena, saw in the statutes an assault on the Jewishness of Jesus (and his mother) that compromised the essential character of Christianity itself.[47] Those without pure Spanish blood, the new argument ran, could not be trusted in high office because of an innate tendency to sink into infidelity. They were inferior by nature. While there is no direct historical relationship between this early example of both ideological and institutional racism in European history and its twentieth-century counterparts, the appearance of such a doctrine in Christian society was a sinister portent of things to come. What was believable in the fifteenth century became even more plausible in succeeding centuries when science made its services available to those who wished to distinguish between the "human breeds" as one distinguishes between various breeds of dogs and horses.

THE ENLIGHTENMENT AND ITS AFTERMATH

Another question raised by the new age of discovery was fraught with religious implications of even greater moment; perhaps the different types of humanity were simply too different to be reduced to a common denominator. Perhaps – a heretical notion – humankind was not descended, as the Bible claimed, from a single set of parents – Adam and Eve – after all. Monogenesis, on which human unity essentially depended, slowly came under suspicion, although even European writers of a sceptical bent were reluctant to break openly with Christian orthodoxy until the secular Enlightenment was in full flower and scepticism was in vogue.

Nevertheless, the drift toward polygenesis began, assisted by a growing scientific passion for the classification of data that reached its peak with Carl von Linnaeus (1707–78) and Johann Friedrich Blumenbach (1752–1840). Inevitably, the classifying instinct fanned the embers of racial speculation into a more vibrant glow. Moreover, medieval cosmology, quite apart from any ideas contributed by anti-biblical scepticism, supplied a convenient model for organizing newly acquired anthropological data into a static hierarchical system. Not only did the "Great Chain of Being" rest on the principle of hierarchy, but, according to Plotinus, its neo-Platonic originator, a rational world must exhibit every mode of imperfection through its creatures.[48] "If all other created beings were ranked upon a grand scale," Jordan comments, "why not man?"[49] Conceivably, the same principle could be applied and the human species graded "from its noblest specimens to its most brutal savages."[50] When white Europeans compared themselves with non-white non-Europeans, the potential for a new chain of being was immense. Predictably, the classifiers located themselves at the top of the scale; from their perspective, no other procedure was possible.

On this theory, the Creator had even provided an index according to colour and other assorted physical traits (colour was not the only consideration in the new epoch) to assist his most noble specimens in their task of classification. Before the birth of Christianity, Aristotle had correlated the shape of the forehead, eyebrows, nose, and colour of the eyes to the human temperament; this was extremely helpful to later ages. [51] Facial angles were also regarded as significant by the ancients. Did not the Greek sculptors represent the superhuman attributes of their gods by giving them "a facial angle of 100 degrees, exceeding that of the highest human?"[52] It was the Dutch anatomist Peter Camper (1722–89) who revived this simple means of determining human intelligence, with all its hierarchical implications. "It is amusing to contemplate," Camper declared, "an arrangement of [skulls], placed in a regular succession: apes, orangs, negroes, the skull of an Hottentot, Madagascar, Chinese, Moguller, Calmuck, and divers Europeans."[53] To the eighteenth-century mind, the progression was obvious and the case for human unity (and human distinctiveness *vis-à-vis* animals) weakened. Nevertheless, the rise of racism cannot be attributed to these scientific trends alone, nor to their polygenetic innuendoes. There were other avenues to the same destination, and some of them did not require so great a departure from more orthodox convictions. Another look at the subject of slavery confirms this observation.

Neither monogenesis nor Christian universalism were able to hinder racial oppression and the lucrative slave trade. To be sure, polygenesis, or the theory of multiple human origins, was a more congenial rationale for enslaving non-whites, but the same end could be accomplished without breaking the thread of human unity by a racial interpretation of Noah's curse on the children of Ham. When blacks were finally enslaved by white Europeans at the threshold of the modern era, their fate could be justified as the decree of a wise and beneficent providence. Not only had God placed on Ham's descendants the "black mark" of condemnation and servitude for their ancestor's sin, but God had actually done so for their own spiritual welfare. [54] The colonial masters did not require Aristotle after all; the Bible supplied a sufficient and wholly Christian foundation for the institution of black slavery on the part of the European nations, particularly the Protestant nations with their faith in *sola scriptura*: the efficacy of God's word.

In colonial America, the same biblical myth could be adapted to account for the role of the Indians in the Christian dispensation. Was not Japheth, the archetypal white, destined to dwell in the tents of Shem as well as to enslave (for their own good) the children of Ham? The progressive usurpation of Indian territories with the expansion of the colonial frontier made this view extremely appealing.[55] Japheth was literally moving into the tents of Shem. With the more rationalistic believers, for whom biblical myths no longer possessed the credibility required for this kind of immediate application, it was always possible to suggest a polygenist perspective within a monogenist framework by arguing that God had created other races before Adam's offspring (the pre-Adamites), and that these races, being inferior by design, could be enslaved.[56] Through science or through scripture, the consciences of the slave-traders and slave-owners were assuaged, although a few, like Thomas Jefferson, trembled before the prospect of divine justice. This fear, however, did not prevent the author of the Declaration of Independence from believing in white superiority.[57]

The Enlightenment philosophers were thorough-going sceptics. Scorning the Bible as a bundle of superstitious fables, they mocked the biblical account of creation and turned to more radical ideas, which they frequently combined with pronounced racial sentiments. Here, for example, are David Hume's reflections on race:

I am apt to suspect the negroes and in general all the other species of men (for there are four or five different kinds) to be naturally inferior to the whites. There never was a civilized nation of any other complexion than white, nor even any individual eminent either in action or speculation. No ingenious manufactures amongst them, no arts, no sciences. On the other hand, the most rude and barbarous of the whites, such as the ancient GERMANS, the present TARTARS, have still something eminent about them, in their valour, form of government, or some other particular. Such a uniform and constant difference could not happen in so many countries and ages, *if nature had not made an original distinction betwixt these breeds of men*. Not to mention our colonies, there are NEGROE slaves dispersed all over EUROPE, of which none ever discovered any symptoms of ingenuity, tho' low people, without education, will start up amongst us, and distinguish themselves in every profession. In JAMAICA indeed they talk of one negroe as a man of parts and learning; but 'tis likely he is admired for very slender accomplishments like a parrot, who speaks a few words plainly.[58] [Italics mine.]

Why did Hume allow his great critical intelligence to sink to this dismal level? Not, according to Richard Popkin, because of an idiosyncratic prejudice peculiar to the Scottish philosopher alone,[59] although, according to another commentator, his radical empiricism may have played a part in his racial denigration of blacks since Hume believed that "man is as he appears," and, to the vast majority of whites, blacks appeared to be stupid.[60] Hume's thought was flawed because the Age of Reason itself was flawed, suffering from the same deep-seated ethnocentric bias as an older Christendom and a still older classical civilization. Like their predecessors, Enlightenment thinkers were not aware of their bias. Even when human nature was defined in universal, rational terms, it was always possible to restrict the essence of humanity to one's own kinship group or cultural matrix simply by redefining the boundaries of rationality. Thus, certain peoples were excluded from the full possession of reason on some pretext or other, usually connected with displeasing physical traits that seemed, if one regarded the flesh as an emblem of the soul, to indicate a serious deficiency.

Being white themselves, the Europeans regarded whiteness of skin as intrinsic to normative humanity, so that non-whiteness necessarily subtracted from the inner as well as the outer state of true human existence. It implied either sickness or degeneracy or both, caused, perhaps, by the ill effects of an unsatisfactory climate or diet over a sustained period of time; so, at any rate, Count Buffon decided.[61] This disorder was bound to damage the rational faculty and thereby the general potential of its victims. Entire races, in other words, could be seen in much the same light as mentally deficient individuals, and, by implication, should be treated accordingly. Furthermore, to some eighteenth-century writers, not everyone who looked human really was human: some actually belonged lower down on the creaturely scale between *Homo sapiens* and the apes. Other thinkers adopted the pre-Adamite interpretation, declaring that the species created prior to Adam never possessed the traits of genuine humanity in the first place.[62] In this way, it was possible to blame God for their inequality, assuming that one still believed in God and in the notion of Creation itself.

Pre-Adamite doctrines were immensely influential. They outlived their Enlightenment apologists and acquired considerable prestige in the early nineteenth century, especially in the United States. Notable in this respect was the American paleontologist Samuel Morton (1799–1841), a pre-evolutionary scientist who, like his British contemporary Robert Knox, was preoccupied with the anatomical foundations (and proofs) of human inequality.[63] Morton believed not only that the different races had different origins, but that the race with the largest cranium – the Caucasion (white or Adamic) – had, for that reason, "a decided and unquestionable superiority."[64] Evidently, larger heads contained bigger brains and bigger brains contained better minds, or so it was assumed. On this assumption, Morton demonstrated the higher intelligence of the Adamites over the pre-Adamites by arranging his five basic races on a descending scale according to the quantity of lead-shot required to fill the skulls of each type.[65] Predictably, the negroid skulls in his collection (known as the American Golgotha) were discovered to possess the smallest cranial capacity.

As evolutionary ideas were not yet current, racial judgments by Morton and various other physical anthropologists acquired a fixed and static character that rendered them all the more intractable in (ante-bellum) America, a society that was rapidly entering a period of social and political crisis. One did not need to call upon the curse of Ham to oppose the cause of black emancipation; modern science, at least in the hands of social conservatives, was equally effective. When the famous paleontologist died in 1851, he was eulogized as "one of the brightest ornaments of our age and country," and in the south as a man who had contributed "most materially in giving to the negro his true position as an inferior race."[66] Unwittingly, Morton and his pre-Darwinian associates merely employed new scientific techniques to confirm the white ethnocentric convictions that they had received intact from the Enlightenment. By 1850, as Nancy Stepan has pointed out, racial science was "far less universalistic, egalitarian and humanistic in its outlook than it had been in 1800."[67] In light of this transformation, it was no accident that neither Morton nor his fellow scientists in America had serious moral difficulties with the institution of black slavery. Nor, for that matter, did many churchmen.

With increasing support for white supremacy from the new science, both America and Europe started to teeter on the edge of the racist precipice. The omens were clear, and the emergence of racism as a discernible and definable radical worldview only awaited the rise of Darwinism, the crystallization of the Aryan race myth, and the peculiar mood of the late nineteenth century. Slowly and inexorably a metamorphosis was taking place that, once realized, would shatter a host of humane values from the rich store of Western ethics: Stoic natural law, New Testament brotherly love, Roman jurisprudence, medieval Scholasticism, Renaissance humanism, Catholic and Protestant spirituality, Kantian morality, and democratic idealism. All the various threads previously described were eventually gathered into the fabric of racist ideology: ethnocentric pride, colour dualism, physical contrast, religious symbolism, biblical exegesis, theological exposition, purity of blood imagery, scientific classification, poly-genesis, craniometry, as well as many other elements that have not been mentioned (including evolutionary theory).

A complete account is neither possible nor necessary in these pages. Even if such an account were provided, however, the subject would not thereby be exhausted for, like all ideologies, racism is always more than the sum of its components. A worldview, since it supplies a point of departure for thought in general, soon acquires a transcendent significance, especially when it seeks – as racism does – to diagnose the ills of mortal life and human history and prescribe their cure. The racist who appeared in America and Europe before the end of the nineteenth century was a typical ideologue; he knew that he possessed a higher wisdom: a new ethic grounded in a new law of nature that represented at once the true foundation of all science, all philosophy, and all religion. In that sense, racism must be distinguished from the racial ethnocentrism that preceded its rise, but, since no historical phenomenon is conceived without antecedents, it was also intertwined with certain key events in Western history that served as catalysts for far-reaching changes in the mental horizon of the heirs of European civilization. Of these events, the establishment of the great colonial empires was undoubtedly the most significant. Ruth Benedict saw this almost thirty years ago. "Racism did not get its currency in modern thought until it was applied to conflicts within Europe ... But it is possible to wonder whether the doctrine would have been proposed at all ... if the basis for it had not been laid in the violent experience of racial prejudice on the frontier."[68]

RACISM AMONG THE "ISMS"

The term "racism" was apparently coined in the 1930s against the background of the German Third Reich.[69] It would not have occurred to last-century elaborators of racial theory to apply such a label to either their opinions or their persons. In this respect, they were different from the authors of the related term "antisemitism" (An-tisemitismus) in imperial Germany, who wore their new designation with pride.[70] But this difference is beside the point. Racism, like its variant antisemitism, is an "ism," a distinctive doctrine to which a distinctive agenda has been attached – one with political implications. In fact, since its genesis, racism has been among the most powerful and dangerous isms of the modern world.

The suffix "ism," however, is insufficient to describe its character. Racism is also an ideology in most of the various meanings of that vexing term, including visionary speculation, utopian myth, social and class bias, an intellectual schema, and the official creed of a movement. If a single aspect of life, or one of its essential components, is regarded as the whole of life, or at least as its fundamental cornerstone, an ideology is born: that is, a mode of interpretation in which the intrinsic sense of the dominant idea is applied in all possible directions until everything in history and human experience is subsumed under its logic.[71] The idea of race is such an idea: hence *racism* (or racialism, as it is sometimes called). Racism, however, did not rise alone but in conjunction with a number of other isms, notably liberalism, nationalism, Marxism, and fascism, and its emergence on the stage of the modern world must be understood as part of a more general *Zeitgeist* than a narrow account of the development of racial thought suggests. It is to this larger context of the subject we now turn.

All the formidable ideas and political systems that constitute the great ideologies of our age are quite recent. Liberalism, for example, was the product of the eighteenth-century Enlightenment with some nineteenth-century modifications. Nationalism, as the term is understood today, only dates back to the French Revolution (1789), when, for the first time, the concept of the nation as a collective and mystical unity found passionate expression in the historical arena, and a national hymn – *La Marseillaise* – and national flag – *le tricolore* – replaced the former dynastic symbols.[72] (Patriotism, on the other hand, is an ancient emotion, and not to be confused with nationalism.[73]) Marxism, or radical socialism, and racism are the offspring of the mid-nineteenth century, and fascism, a special form of nationalism, is really the child of the twentieth century.

The recent emergence of these concepts indicates that the modern age unleashed not only ideas but also feelings that had not been present, or present only in an embryonic sense, in the pre-modern period.[74] Clearly, some kind of larger revolution involving the mental and spiritual realms was necessary before these new forces could be born. Whatever else it entails, modernity – the concepts governing our contemporary intellectual vision – rests indisputably on secular foundations, and secularism, i.e., the stress on this-worldliness (Latin: *saeculum*), appeared as the Age of Reason succeeded the Age of Faith in one of the great watersheds of Western culture. These "ages," of course, are arbitrary designations; nonetheless, such transitions do occur and are invariably accompanied by considerable anxiety and trepidation. Why did the end of the Age of Faith allow a surge of dynamic new concepts, each with its own social agenda, to engulf the European spirit?

The English historian of ideas Michael Biddiss argues that the secular notions of nation, class, and race arose out of the shattered pieces of medieval Christian unity after its destruction both by Protestantism, with its centrifugal tendencies, and by the later acids of eighteenth-century scepticism.[75] In other words, certain ideas, usually associated with the identities of groups, that otherwise might never have found an independent place in social speculation, were pushed to the forefront of modern thought by virtue of this dissolution. Each in due course became, for certain persons, the key to history itself. The Enlightenment philosophers, for example, isolated the concept of the individual, which, although scarcely a group idea *per se*, generated the collective doctrine of the "rights of man" dear to the hearts of liberals past and present. More to the point, Johann-Gottlieb Fichte and his German romantic contemporaries made the concept of the nation paramount; Karl Marx and his fellow socialists isolated the concept of class; Count Arthur de Gobineau and a few others emphasized the concept of race.

The disintegration of a unified and transcendent scheme of things in which earth and heaven were closely joined in a single intellectual and religious vision made it relatively easy for the modern mind to regard one or other of the fragments of the old cosmos as a new centre of sacred meaning. These ideas gradually assumed the character of ideologies, thus gaining a transcendence of their own. As ideologies, moreover, they were soon swept into the maelstrom of modern politics because they were useful in the power struggles of the age, supplying those who employed them with a profound sense of who they were and where they belonged in the social order. This usefulness explains why the idea of race acquired a new and unprecedented significance in the nineteenth century as the basis of the ideology of racism. As we will see later, Count Gobineau was a crucial figure in this development.

Théophile Simar, a Belgian author of an older generation, blamed the rise of racism on the decline of traditional religious belief as defined by the Catholic Middle Ages. To Simar, the collapse of the beautiful, ordered, and rational universe of medieval Christian faith was responsible for a mighty tide of evils. Modern philosophy and theology, detached from their familiar metaphysical moorings (the Great Chain of Being), plunged into such dark eddies as nominalism, vitalism, subjectivism, and materialism.[76] Racism, in his eyes, was not the logical extension of a hierarchical understanding of creation; instead, it was the natural fruit and final consequence of theories that interpreted life as perpetual flux and chaotic motion, and that celebrated extreme diversity, everlasting struggle, and endless becoming. Once these bold new conceptions were released into the bloodstream of the modern age, they poisoned a substantial segment of its thought, leaving the remainder in a weakened condition. As a result, the notions of structure, stability, and harmony were no longer effective; after the eighteenth century, according to Simar, they virtually disappeared from the European intellectual perspective, the *coup de grâce* having been administered by radical anti-religious thinkers such as Nietzsche and Darwin.[77] Influenced by Protestantism, agnosticism, atheism, and nihilism, the children of modernity became the prey of highly relativistic interpretations of reality that left them vulnerable to extreme and potentially dangerous social views. It is scarcely surprising, therefore, that so many people in the nineteenth and twentieth centuries attached themselves so readily to ideas that seemed to bestow some meaning on the flux, some order on the chaos, and some purpose on the struggle.

The idea of race was such an idea. Racism was a tragic product of modernity; it represented the ambiguous and finally sinister side of the disintegration of what was once a great Christian cosmology, and its manifestation was fraught with peril for the future of humanity. The same could be said of nationalism, the first cousin of racism and another spinoff of the romantic, subjectivistic mood that Simar disliked so much in the Protestant and ex-Protestant German philosophers after Fichte. Simar's conclusions, of course, were exaggerated, but, in spite of the Catholic bias so evident throughout his study, he knew that racism could not be understood apart from the mental and spiritual revolution that shattered the traditional symbols of religious transcendence and paved the way for the formation of secular religions in their stead. If God is abolished, something else will play God's role.

The phase "secular religion" seems a contradiction in terms. Perhaps it is, but it is difficult to deny that the great modern isms contain a religious element, even when they assume an anti-religious posture. This element appears in the typical demand for submission to the "truth" uttered by every ideologue, for truth implies ultimacy, and religion, if the Protestant theologian Paul Tillich's famous definition is sound, implies "ultimate concern."[78] It is no coincidence that the major isms of the West have been couched in cosmic or religious language such as dialectical materialism or the sacred mission (manifest destiny) of the nation or the divinity of Aryan man. Yet such secular or "quasi-religions" (to employ another of Tillich's terms) are not true religions.[79] They do not arise as responses to profound religious experiences or encounters with the numinous, but merely as ideas that, as a consequence of their social utility, have caught fire in the crucible of the modern consciousness. Nevertheless, their power is in some measure a religious power for they excite strong feelings and can hold multitudes in their thrall. For this reason, they do not perish easily; otherwise, because of their inherent fragility, we would surely have witnessed their final *Götterdämmerung*.

No one has described the religious nature of the fixed idea raised to an absolute degree more vividly than Jean-Paul Sartre, for whom antisemitism was a "passion" and the antisemite a modern "Manichaen" – a "holy man."[80] For Sartre, at the core of the anti-Jewish ideology of the European racists during the Nazi and post-Nazi eras resided a burning desire to defeat the cosmic powers of darkness which, tragically, the new "Knight-errant of the Good" perceived as incarnate in the Jew.[81] Insofar as the great isms of the modern age have awakened this measure of ultimate concern, they cannot be regarded as devoid of a religious dimension, whatever the exact nature of their creeds.

If this analysis is correct, a further point must be added before I can return to my central theme. In dealing with the secular religions, we are dealing not merely with ideas but also with myths. Myths are intrinsically religious and arise as certain tales in a given culture assume a larger-than-life significance: "stories that tell a society what is important for it to know, whether about its gods, its history, its laws, or its class structure.[82] They arise because something in these narratives resonates with something in the society during critical moments in its formation and development. In its own way, a myth explains things and answers fundamental questions, especially questions concerning human origins and the riddle of evil in the world. Nor are myths merely creatures of the past, remnants of the dim and distant twilight era of the human odyssey; there are modern myths as well.

Indeed, as Tillich once declared, it is useful to distinguish between archaic and modern myths, or between myths that belong to the pre-literate and pre-critical stages of the human consciousness and those that belong to its post-critical stages.[83] The latter stages, of course, saw the rise of science as well as increased emphasis on reason; one of the problems with any discussion of the nature of myth is that, as far as the rationalistic and scientific mind is concerned, the term is synonymous with fable rather than with truth. Paradoxically, therefore, modern myths have been forced to present themselves as science, for "myth is believable on autonomous soil only in scientific guise."[84] Only in this respect, however, are modern myths different from archaic myths. Performing the same functions and answering the same questions, they seem rooted in the myth-making faculty of the human psyche which never loses its ingenuity in the manufacture of new myths if deprived of old ones.

Each of the important isms that has arisen in western history in modern times reveals a mythic core. Classical liberalism, for example, with its roots in eighteenth-century axioms concerning human and historical perfectibility, affirms the myth of infinite progress. Nationalism never fails to invoke particular myths of national origin potent enough to unite the nation around common symbols. Fascism invariably superimposes racism on nationalism, changing the myth of national origin into a myth of racial supremacy. Classical Marxism, which is fond of calling itself historical science, is clearly mythic in its depictions of pre-history and post-history: the communist societies of beginning-time and end-time. Classical racism also possesses an audacious myth, the Aryan myth, the great race myth of the white Europeans, which, in a variety of expressions, managed to dominate the cultural ethos of the most powerful nations in the Western world, including the Americas.

THE ARYAN MYTH

The Aryan myth is a modern myth. As such, it is a product of the modern mind and the age of science. Obviously, science can mean a host of subjects as well as a body of methods and principles: biology, anthropology, archaeology, linguistic studies, sociology, psychology, chemistry, physics, etc. The Aryan myth is an artful compound of most of the former (except the physical sciences) in addition to being a narrative concerning primordial time and the sacred origins of the human race. Like all true myths, it is a tale of good and evil and the perennial contest between these opposing forces in the arena of nature and history. Not only does it answer existential questions, but its emergence during a time of crisis in Western society had momentous consequences for modernity as a whole. The background of this crisis – the loss of transcendence as the Age of Faith gave way to the Age of Reason – has already been described. According to Carl Jung, abandoning religious faith created a dangerous vacuum in the European soul, prompting a quest for a new religious myth in order that the world might "draw upon fresh spiritual resources and renew its creative powers.[85] The Aryan myth filled this vacuum, for, as Mircea Eliade has written, behind it beats the passion for noble origin that all humans feel.[86]

The Aryan was really an Adamic figure; he was at once both "the 'primordial' Ancestor and the noble 'hero'" – the "exemplary model that must be imitated in order to recover racial 'purity,' physical strength, nobility, [and] the heroic 'ethics' of the glorious and creative 'beginnings.'"[87] Possessing all the attributes that the modern Europeans felt they lacked, and which they desperately craved, in their eyes the mythical Aryan was a healing symbol who could restore the lost vitality and marvellous energies of youth. This was the main secret of his appeal in the nineteenth and twentieth centuries when industrial civilization suddenly seemed soulless and exhausted to many Europeans, particularly those who, for personal reasons, were out of joint with their times. The Aryan appealed to others, too, of course, since the myth acquired great popularity and not all Europeans (or Americans) suffered from Jung's spiritual vacuum. But the need for a new Adam was its galvanizing force. In the succeeding chapters, we shall explore this mood more closely.

The Aryan myth had simple origins. Philology, the academic study of language, whose students were "as innocent as innocent can be" of racism, coined the fateful terms "Aryan" and "Semite" during the eighteenth century.[88] The tale is familiar. Sir William Jones, an English jurist in newly conquered British India, became interested in Sanskrit and quickly realized its grammatical affinities with Latin and Greek. (Like all upper-class Englishmen, he had enjoyed the benefits of a sound classical education.) This induced others to posit a linguistic relationship between the Greek, Latin, Persian, and Sanskrit languages as distinguished from the Hebrew-related or Semitic languages. This presumed that the so-called Indo-European languages had a common linguistic ancestor, a notion that at once became popular in Europe where scholarship had hitherto shown little interest in non-European languages (except Hebrew). From the *Histories* (Book 7) of Herodotus, the Greek historian of antiquity, came the word "Arian" (Aryan), originally employed as a designation for the Medes and Persians but now applied to all the Indo-European peoples. The term "Semite," from Shem, one of the sons of Noah, was applied to the Hebrew family (Phoenician, Aramaic, Syriac, etc.) possibly by the philosopher Gottfried Wilhelm Leibniz, (If this is the case, its coinage was earlier and of independent origin.) The contrast between the two linguistic groups was strongly accentuated.

At first, however, this contrast was purely philological, but what began as a distinction between linguistic groups soon became an ethnic and finally a racial distinction under the aegis of romanticism, whose currents swept through the salons of the later eighteenth and early nineteenth centuries. According to the romantics, language and life are bound together in an organic unity. If language truly flows out of the subterranean depths of life, then each tongue will surely reflect the spiritual character of the particular people or nation that utters its sounds and syllables. Johann Gottfried Herder, Friedrich Schlegel, Johann-Gottlieb Fichte, and other German *literati* thought more or less in this fashion. So evidently did Christian Lassen, a Bonn professor and follower of Schlegel, and Max Müller, later a Sanskrit scholar and an Oxford professor.[89]

These men of letters, besides falling in love with such esoteric ideas, also fell in love with the past, sinking especially under the romantic spell of "Mother India," the supposed home of Aryanism and the imaginary womb of civilization itself. It was not a large step for most of them to conceive of a racial kinship between the white Europeans and an original white (i.e., Aryan) race whose place of genesis was ancient India, indeed, the Himalayas themselves. This original race was believed to have marched down from the "roof of the world" in long columns of "masterful men," founding empires and civilizations in its wake.[90]

The Aryans, common source of the European peoples, were idealized and hallowed. They became the children of nature, singing, living, fighting, without social conventions ... The Aryans, who condemned unions with the vanquished, had therefore a sense of racial value and of the sacredness of blood ... One established therefore a causal relation between the splendour of Brahmanic culture and its respect for purity of blood ... There was never the least doubt; the Aryans formed the predestined race charged with the mission of bearing the light in the world.[91]

These torch-bearers of the great light of civilization were the ancestors of the modern Europeans, who were swiftly grafted onto the ancient tree. In particular, they were held to be the ancestors of the Germans, and the Germans were the ancestors of the proper rulers of France and Britain. The German connection was significant: like the primordial Aryans, the early Germans were regarded with special favour by the romantics, and one did not have to be German to share this admiration. It was a Germanophile Frenchman, Count Arthur de Gobineau (1816–82) who, in his famous *Essai sur l'inégalité des races humaines* (1853–5), gave the Aryan myth its definitive form.

Human history is like an immense tapestry. The earth is the frame over which it is stretched. The successive centuries are the tireless weavers. As soon as they are born they immediately seize the shuttle and operate it on the frame, working at it until they die. The broad fabic thus goes on growing beneath their busy fingers. The two most inferior varieties of the human species, the black and yellow races, are the crude foundation, the cotton and wool, which the secondary families of the white group make supple by adding their silk; while the Aryan group, circling its finer threads through the noble generations, designs on its surface a dazzling masterpiece of arabesques in silver and gold ...[92]

Intelligent, virile, freedom-loving, creative, and virtuous, the magnificent Aryan was really Gobineau himself, at least as he saw himself, as well as the image of his social class. Thus the Europeans flattered themselves, regarding their own racial lineage as the *summum bonum* of the entire historical process and the key to its meaning. Silver and gold are more beautiful than cotton and wool, and the Aryan race, if Gobineau is to be believed, is more beautiful than the yellow and black races or else it could not be superior. This notion was the legacy of the European Renaissance, when, along with other aspects of classical culture, Greek aesthetic ideas were elevated to the status of eternal principles, producing a model for the most perfect, i.e., most beautiful, human form: a model that the nineteenth-century racists adopted and internalized in order to distinguish the higher and lower races.[93] The straight nose, the broad forehead, the correct facial angle, the clear intelligent eyes, the athletic body suggesting harmony and balance (both inner and outer), and, of course, whiteness of skin, were all features of this ideal.

With such a self-portrait, it is not strange that the white European, like Narcissus in the old Greek fable, became intoxicated with his own image and its reflection in the waters of time. Eros is excited by beauty, and the extraordinary physical attraction of the noble figure created by the "father of racist ideology"[94] and the other authors of Aryan splendour was irresistible to those who were fortunate enough to belong to his line. Had they paid more attention to classical mythology, however, the makers of the Aryan myth might have learned an invaluable lesson: Narcissus was punished when his self-infatuation turned into a death-snare.

THE RACIST ERA

The racist era in Western history began in the latter half of the nineteenth century and ended – to the extent that it *has* ended – with the collapse of the German Third Reich in 1945, although its golden age, according to Pierre van den Berghe, was between 1880 and 1920.[95] It began when the Aryan myth started to colour the scientific, philosophical, artistic, political, and religious thought of the modern world, casting its shadow over the entire cultural land-scape: music, classical studies, literature – nothing escaped. It began in Europe when anti-Judaism evolved into antisemitism, when eco-nomic systems were defined as "Semitic" or "Aryan," when nationality was endowed with a racial meaning, when military victory or defeat was made to hinge on skull-shapes or cranial indices, when religion was seen as an expression of race, and, in the Christian church, when theology permitted its central ideas and symbols, including Jesus himself, to be recast in a racist mould. It began in post-bellum America when anti-reconstructionists drew on both old and new race doctrines, including those imported from the far side of the Atlantic Ocean, in order to disenfranchise the recently enfranchised blacks on the grounds of racial inferiority.[96] It began when, as Simar indicated, the concept of race satisfied all the ravenous appetites of the age: pan-Germanism, Anglo-Saxon expansionism, French na-tionalism and cultural imperialism, and the thirst for proof that the white peoples of the earth had a great and glorious destiny.[97]

Writers in many fields, but especially in the social sciences, became infatuated with the new popular enthusiasm; a tremendously for-midable ideology was taking shape in their hands. It was possible, for example, for a French author to interpret the first world war from a "bio-psychological" perspective borrowed from Gobineau, whose *Essai* had allegedly allowed the contemporary generation to grasp the principles of "ethno-mytho-bio-psychology" and thereby to understand the underlying factors in the current struggle.[98] The fact that such a peculiar blend of science, myth, and fantasy could even have been published during this period, and have been taken seriously to boot, reveals the extent to which racism had captured the public mind.

When the National Socialist state was reduced to rubble in the second world war, the Aryan myth that had inspired its founders suffered a similar fate as far as society at large was concerned. Sud-denly, the remarkable credibility that it had enjoyed for almost a century was shattered, and a chapter in the history of ideas came to an apparent end. The horrors of Auschwitz, that grisly monument to the ideology of race, convinced the majority of people in the democratic West that, as Alexis de Tocqueville had seen a very long time ago, such doctrines were pernicious as well as false, and, if translated into a mass forum, would inflict terrible harm on the world.[99] Unfortunately, the demise of the Aryan myth – Aryan lan-guage still survives on the political fringes – did *not* mean that racism itself had disappeared from post-war society. In the judgment of Pierre Paraf, the "power and complexity of the racist phenomenon does not allow us to hope that it was totally effaced, even in the most crushing of defeats."[100] Hence, while in a narrow sense the racist era has ended, in a broad sense it continues in other forms today. South African racism, as we shall see, owes relatively little to the philosophy of Count Gobineau (although Afrikaner thought has other roots in the European intellectual tradition); nevertheless, it remains alive and virulent in the late twentieth century. Nor is it the only case – the monster is hydra-headed.

CHAPTER TWO

The Germanic Christ

It is ironic that a Roman republican of the first century, who was far more interested in the Romans than in the Germans and only wished to remind the former of their lost virtues by praising the tribesmen of the Rhineland frontier, should have become the *de facto* godparent of German racism. Even prior to the rediscovery of Tacitus and his *Germania* by German humanists during the Renaissance, however, a German ethnocentrism with racial overtones was beginning to brew. Through a peculiar manuscript entitled *The Book of a Hundred Chapters*, a racial mythology based on the rejection of the Old Testament, the Mosaic Law, and the teachings of Jesus found its way into the German psyche of the late Middle Ages, although its influence was either non-existent or extremely restricted.[1] Strangely, the unknown author of this unpleasant and highly xenophobic writing called his new "Germanic" religion "Christianity," whereas, as Norman Cohn has declared, its true affinity can be affixed in almost prophetic terms to the National Socialist tracts of Alfred Rosenberg and Walther Darré, not to mention such men as Jakob Wilhelm Hauer, the founder of the racist German Faith Movement (Deutsche Glaubensbewegung) and Hans F.K. Günther.[2] For this reason, *The Book of a Hundred Chapters* is more than a mere historical curiosity; it is indicative of an early tendency on the part of certain Germans to turn away from cosmopolitanism in favour of the exclusively Germanic in the cultural, religious, national, and racial spheres. Its "pan-German eschatology," according to Poliakov, "was certainly not invented out of nothing."[3] Such extremism must have had social roots.

However this conclusion should not be overstated. Neither nationalism nor racism existed in the Middle Ages. Even Martin Luther, although he shared the general antipathy of his German contemporaries toward an oppressive Italian papacy and became a national figure in his confrontation with Charles V at the Diet of Worms, cannot be called a German nationalist. No genuine trace of tribalistic, nationalistic, or racialistic ideology appears in Luther's thought;[4] even his notorious anti-Judaism, although excessive for his day, was religious rather than racial: a compound of medieval superstitious fears concerning Jews and Luther's own evangelical assumptions concerning the meaning of scripture and the forthcoming apocalypse – all coloured by personal choler.[5] Nor has Lutheranism *in its proper sense* ever played more than a minor role in the rise of later German nationalism.[6]

Nevertheless, most post-Reformation German Protestant theology and popular piety has been deeply embedded in German cultural ethnocentrism, including the Lutheran tradition itself, especially since the early nineteenth century. Romanticism, the womb of both nationalism and racism, was responsible for pointing the character of German Protestantism in a nationalistic and racialistic direction, with tragic consequences in the twentieth century. Nations, the romantics believed, are like individuals – indeed, are larger-than-life individuals – and their collective personalities are fully as distinct. This "ontological sophism," as Simar called it,[7] became so firmly accepted during the modern era that even those Germans who still clung to cosmopolitan principles often yielded to its sway.[8] Liberalism was no armour against nationalism, nor was universalism a warranty against feelings of moral superiority, as both classical and modern civilization have demonstrated more than once in Western history.

In the German case, that a liberal theologian, Otto Piper, even during the Nazi period, and even when he was forced to leave Germany, nevertheless defined German theology as an intellectual and spiritual quest for a synthesis between the Christian faith and the "German soul," simply confirms this point.[9] No admirer of the extreme aberrations of German nationalism, Piper was still nationalistic enough to glorify three great moments in German cultural history when this synthesis was supposedly realized: 1 German religious mysticism of the fourteenth century (Meister Eckhart); 2 the German Reformation of the sixteenth century (Luther); 3 the "German Movement" of the late eighteenth- and early nineteenth-centuries (Fichte).[10]

Luther, however, was at the pinnacle of this synthesis. The Reformation, in Piper's view, was as much a German as a Christian event, and could only have transpired through "a person whose individual life is at the same time a significant expression of his nationality."[11] It was Luther's German soul, his profound German soul, that was the true source of his religious wisdom and immense creative powers. This conclusion was the direct product of latter-day romanticism; it would hardly have occurred to Luther himself. Piper, of course, unlike the so-called "German Christian" theologians of the Third Reich, did not wish the notion that creativity and profundity always rest on national and perhaps racial foundations to be carried too far. This is clear from his condemnation of the "German Christian" synthesis between Christianity and Germanism (i.e., National Socialism) as no true synthesis at all but a blatant racialization of the Christian faith and thus its implicit denial. The great Luther, a true German (Hitler was a false German), had balanced Christianity and the German spirit successfully, whereas the late Lutherans, seduced by the Nazi revolution, had discovered only Luther's "German soul" but missed the "beating of his Christian heart."[12] In this judgment, Piper was certainly correct.

That the German soul had been inserted into Christian theology, and the religious insights of the father of the Protestant Reformation linked to his national and racial nature, was proof that Lutheranism in Germany had undergone a metamorphosis since the sixteenth century. Placing a Germanic halo around Luther's head, canonizing him as a prototypal hero of Germanism, meant that Piper, and others like him, had fallen victim to the romantic dogmas that arose between the sixteenth and twentieth centuries and seemed to supply the basis for the third great synthesis between the Christian faith and the German soul. Could the Reformation have occurred without a German religious hero? Could an epochal spiritual revolution have taken place on other than German soil? Do not the Germans, and the Germans alone, possess as part of their national and racial character a special depth of spirit and quality of soul that qualifies them uniquely as the authors of profound ideas and the progenitors of great movements?

FICHTE AND THE GERMANS

This note was struck with ringing force by Johann-Gottlieb Fichte (1762–1814) in French-occupied Berlin in 1807:

But it was impossible for the existing state of things [i.e., the empty religiosity of pre-Reformation Christendom] to continue once this light [i.e., the renaissance of classical learning] had fallen upon a soul whose religion was truly earnest and concerned about life, when this soul was surrounded by a people to whom it could easily import its more earnest view, and when this people found leaders who cared about its urgent needs ... It was in this way that the light fell upon the soul of the German man, Luther.[13]

One must be careful in citing these words. Fichte, a protégé of Immanuel Kant, was a universalist as well as a particularist and only celebrated the glory of the German spirit because he saw it as the bearer of all general values: the particular in which the universal was for the moment enshrined. Germany, at that time a political if not a cultural fiction, was nevertheless in his view the channel of present and future moral progress for the larger realms of western civilization. If, however the Germans were to fulfill their proper destiny as the custodians of a higher enlightenment, they had to reform their entire educational system along the inspirational lines dictated by Fichte, a man who seems to have cast himself in the role of a modern Plato. In this way, the nation would be prepared for its universal mission. It is, however, the particularist elements in Fichte's *Addresses to the German Nation* that have caused him to be remembered as one of the most important authors, and the first real theoretician, of modern German nationalism.[14] There existed, according to Fichte, an intrinsic connection between the divine life of God and the mysterious inner life of the German nation; a life found somewhere in its collective spiritual depths. Once other nations had also had the same invisible unity, but no longer. Only the Germans, whose genius, like the wings of an eagle "whose mighty body thrusts itself on high," could still soar into the heavenly empyrean; non-Germans, by comparison, were merely earthbound "sylphs."[15] Not content with this analogy, Fichte found another: "So we may say that genius in foreign lands will strew with flowers the well-trodden military roads of antiquity, and weave a becoming robe for that wisdom of life which it will easily take for philosophy. The German spirit, on the other hand, will open up new shafts and bring the light of day into their abysses, and hurl up rocky masses of thoughts, out of which ages to come will build their dwellings."[16] Germany, as a consequence of its unique spirituality, was the elect nation, and one could only infer that this status was due to the special characteristics possessed by the Germans.

Fichte's speeches cannot be understood apart from the dramatic events that prompted him to raise his voice in defiance of the conquering French. Napoleonic imperialism was cultural as well as military, promoting the egalitarian credo of the French Revolution and overturning the feudal and quasi-feudal regimes trapped in its path, including the hapless German principalities and minor kingdoms. Modernity, personified by revolutionary France, was everywhere on the offensive, and Germany, which was far from modern, was deeply threatened by the new prometheanism. So, at least, German intellectuals such as Fichte persuaded themselves as they sounded the clarion blast to their embattled compatriots. "Napoleon was taken by hostile Germans less as the symbol of dictatorship than as the symbol of the French Revolution's rationalism, liberalism and legalism, as introduced into Germany by the Code Napoléon."[17] As a reaction to the French intrusion, German romanticism began to turn on a chauvinistic axis, causing even men who owed their preeminence to Enlightenment wisdom (such as Fichte) to turn against the language and culture of the French *philosophes* as the quintessence of superficiality and emptiness. While these early German romantics were nationalists rather than racists, their growing obsession with the mystical core of the German people prepared the way for the future. While, in a technical sense, racism was a French and British, rather than German, invention, it had little difficulty sprouting on German soil once its intellectual seeds were imported from France in the latter part of the nineteenth century. In Fichte's day, antisemitism was already the other side of the new Germanism; the stage was set, therefore, for the identification of the Jews (soon to be called Semites) with the rationalism, liberalism, and legalism so closely associated with Napoleonic imperialism, especially as German Jewry was emancipated by the victorious French legions. Pariahs in Christian society, the Jews became pariahs a second time in the same society by becoming a symbol of all the alienating aspects of modernity.

As the only original – today one would say "authentic" – people (Urvolk), – the only Europeans in intimate touch with their own spiritual and racial origins – Fichte's Germans naturally spoke the only original, i.e., authentic, European language (Ursprache).To the romantic imagination, more than anything else, even more than the occupation of a common territory, the possession of a common tongue was the decisive mark of a people or national entity. Language was believed to be the index of spirit, for speech arises out of nature, the abode of divinity that forms and shapes each particular people in its own particular way. Languages are either living or dead, either joined to or separated from their fountainhead in nature (or spirit), the seat of all life. A living language is more than a spoken language, for dead languages are also spoken. Living languages are nourished by life itself, and, as a result, produce an authentic and profound culture. Dead languages, no longer fed by the underground waters of divine life, can only sustain inauthentic and superficial cultures; while they may appear beautiful, their beauty, like the beauty of dried petals from dead flowers, is fragile and easily crumbles into dust. Because the Germans, unlike their enemies, the neo-Latin French, had not sold their Teutonic birthright for Roman pottage, their culture alone remained in close communion with the inexhaustible power of God, whose Spirit animates our spirits. Their knowledge of this miraculous fact, as Fichte reminded them, bound them together in a special bond of affection and kinship – the "Fatherland" – despite their current political fragmentation.

From this emotional base, modern German nationalism began its spectacular rise. *Volk, Nation,* and *Vaterland,* fused into a single transcendental vision, became the basis of a new German ethnocentrism. The seeds of racism, latent in such notions as the theory that the German language captures and reproduces the sounds of German nature, only required a little fertilization to blossom. Already, in the *Addresses,* their fruition is evident.

Wherever a separate language is found, according to Fichte, a separate nation exists; a nation whose political rebirth may require the travail of blood and war.[18] Thus the German who adopts an alien language sullies his racial identity and therefore his personal integrity.[19] Indeed, there is something entirely unnatural in the very act of learning a language other than one's own, although Fichte felt that nations which had ceased to rule themselves had ceased to be real nations and ought to surrender their languages as well as their autonomy. Those who "are too stupid to learn the language of the dominant race" must exclude themselves from public affairs and "condemn themselves to lifelong subjection."[20] (He did not, however, envisage this fate for his fellow Germans who, in his day, were the victims of Napoleonic aggression and French hegemony.) Conversely, the individual who masters his national tongue draws close to his racial ancestors through the primordial medium of speech with its special sensual and racial qualities, i.e., the forest and river noises supposedly imitated by the early Germans (Teutons).

Given these sentiments, Fichte was not contradicting his first principles when he cast doubt on the Jewishness of Jesus. To my knowledge, he was the first serious thinker since Marcion, the gnostic Christian theologian of antiquity, to deny that Jesus was a Jew. In Fichte's opinion, the Fourth Gospel (John), which he regarded as the only reliable account of Christianity, rendered the saviour's racial descent uncertain by failing to supply him with a Davidic genealogy.[21] Fichte considered the Gospel of John alone to be trustworthy because of its mystical and metaphysical character; the other gospels, as far as he was concerned, only contained morality. Following Marcion, Fichte effectively gnosticized much of Johannine theology (especially the divine *Logos*), making John's "true Christianity" agree with his own idealist presuppositions and with the notion of a deified humanity. Thus he distrusted and rejected the concept of creation as a Jewish, not a Christian, concept.[22] The *Logos* that revealed itself in Jesus of Nazareth was the same mysterious *Logos* or divine presence that continues to disclose itself in nature and history, especially German nature and German history. If the Germans were the last authentic people with the last authentic language in Europe, if the German genius soared like an eagle into the empyrean, then the Germans were very much like Jesus, whose spiritual genius also soared into the empyrean – or Jesus was very much like the Germans.

The Jewish genius, on the other hand, most decidedly did *not* soar into the empyrean. How, in that case, could Jesus have been Jewish, when his spirit was so un-Jewish, indeed, so *German?* The hint is clear, although the equation is never made explicit. Paul, of course, who "would not admit that he had been in the wrong in having been once a Jew,"[23] was quite another subject. Fichte died before the terms Aryan and Semite acquired their later racial connotations, and his Jesus, unlike that of Marcion, at least had the merit of remaining a flesh-and-blood human being rather than a gnostic phantom, but he nonetheless represents a decisive step in the construction of a new, antisemitic Christian mythology of nation and race. With his speculations, the Aryanization of Christ was launched.

PIETISM AND ITS NATIONALISTIC
DISTORTIONS

The Christian matrix of national and racial authenticity was crucial to Fichte's thought. Behind this architect of modern German nationalism lay the older religious legacy of German pietism, the greatest post-Reformation movement of spiritual reform in German Christianity whose typical expressions adorned Fichte's speeches.[24] Pietism in religion has frequently been compared to romanticism in literature, art, and music since both the pietists and the romantics drew their inspiration from the experiential and mystical elements in life rather than the purely rational elements. While the original founders of the movement, Philip Jacob Spener and August Francke, cannot be described as German nationalists, their religious ideas, especially their axial doctrine of spiritual rebirth (*Wiedergeburt*), have been identified as a major, although indirect, source of later German nationalism. According to Koppel Pinson's seminal study,[25] it was an easy step to transpose the *Wiedergeburt* from the personal to the social plane of existence, and pietistic Protestants, once contaminated by nationalistic feelings, were prone to take this step. Furthermore, this form of interior religion was closely analogous to nationalism itself.

The Enlightenment or the rationalists conceived of the state or the group as something existing *for* the individual, as something external to him and without any relationship to him other than utilitarian. Nationalism, however, appears with this mystical idea of an *inner* relationship – of some sort of mystical union inherent in all the members of the group which binds them together by force of inner necessity and not merely by accident or for utilitarian motives. Just as Christ is within us … so, according to the nationalist, is nationality within us.[26]

If Christ and nationality are both within us, then Christ and nationality must belong together. Not only did the pietists rebel against the Enlightenment understanding of religion as merely another aspect of universal humanity, regarding it as an "abomination",[27] but they emphasized the particularity of each historic form of the Christian faith. No longer was a universal natural religion detected underneath every particular religion and defined as the real religion of humanity. Instead, Christianity was individualized in much the same way as Germany: religion was a fundamental facet of éach separate cultural and national entity, a part of the living organism of the nation itself. Even in Spener's seventeenth-century classic *Pia Desideria*, where the father of pietism recommends that theological students conduct their disputations in German rather than Latin and devote themselves to the study of German spiritual texts, there is a hint of this future tendency.[28]

However, it was Friedrich Schleiermacher (1768–1834), Fichte's slightly younger contemporary and fellow nationalist, whose political sermons gave German Protestantism a Germanic flavour that theology, as opposed to philosophy, could adopt and exploit. A Hernhutter (Moravian pietist) of a "higher order" who once declared that only Germans were profound enough to appreciate serious religious ideas,[29] Schleiermacher believed in the *Volksstaat*, or state built essentially on *völkisch* or natural principles. If the state and the church are closely intertwined, and if patriotic feeling and religious feeling are closely intermingled, it is difficult to distinguish them – and ultimately unnecessary. As Schleiermacher declaimed from the pulpit during Prussia's struggle with Napoleon, the Christian who lacks loyalty to the Fatherland will "always remain an alien in the house of God."[30]

God, moreover, has imparted to each nation its own distinctive ethos, marking out "bounds and limits for the habitations of the different races of men on the face of the earth."[31] (At one point, Schleiermacher seems to have thought that a single racial origin was the basis of modern nationhood, but he later qualified this view.)[32] Nations, once they have developed to a "certain height," are degraded if they receive foreign elements into their corporate life; to do so is to act in an unnatural fashion.[33] Even "the striving for foreign education is an aberration ... In every foreign institution a different *Gemeingeist* is reflected and the pupil, whose moral and spiritual development should proceed always in relation to his subsequent particular civic activity, will become imbued with an alien instead of a native spirit."[34]

These Fichtean sentiments were intensified by the theologian's pietistic stress on the mystical Johannine doctrine of the spiritual rebirth. Schleiermacher, like Fichte, assigned a special priority to the Fourth Gospel as the most profound of the Gospels. In being born again, we rise to the higher consciousness of our absolute dependence on the eternal, or to God-consciousness, through experience of the indwelling Spirit out of the "impenetrable darkness of divine creation"[35] (unlike Fichte, Schleiermacher was too orthodox to reject the Hebrew concept of creation). When Schleiermacher preached in this vein, he undoubtedly referred mainly to individuals, but his thought contains at least the suggestion that nations might also be the recipients of this spiritual visitation since, from the romantic point of view, they are also individuals. The birth of Christianity was more than a historical metaphor: it signified a radical new beginning for the human race. "And so for every nation the appearing of the gospel is its regeneration, not only a perfecting of its former condition ..."[36] His listeners might well have concluded that the nation, as well as the individual, could be reborn.

With mentors of this calibre – of course, they were not alone – the influence of nationalism on German Protestantism received a powerful impetus. Even the new literary science of higher criticism, which owed so much to German scholarship, became, as Albert Schweitzer noted, deeply infected with Germanic feelings as biblical scholars as well as theologians struggled to reconcile Jesus with Germanism and Germanism with Jesus.[37] Schleiermacher, however, would not have approved of these later trends. On occasion, this struggle moved outside the church. Paul de Lagarde (1827–91), an ex-Christian and fervent admirer of Fichte (for his nationalism), as well as a nationalist prophet in his own right, is one of the best examples. A gifted but warped professor in the field of near eastern languages, Lagarde turned with Nietzschean fury against the orthodox Lutheranism of his childhood, seeing it as a religion contaminated by Judaism and the Christian image of Jesus as an intolerable distortion.[38] For him, in no sense was the true Jesus (to whose figure he remained strangely attached) a Jew. Instead Jesus, for Lagarde, was wholly *sui generis*, an extraordinary genius who, like Copernicus, had turned the world upside down. Why did Jesus choose the designation "Son of Man" for himself? Surely Lagarde suggested, to demonstrate that he was no Jew, but a conscious rebel against Judaism and its precepts. "He [Jesus] calls himself a human being – for that is the meaning of the earlier misunderstood term Son of Man – wanting to be a non-Jew, wanting, we may perhaps add, not to be a member of any one nation, if this nation is proud of its preeminent or exclusive worth ..."[39]

Although this sounds like universalism, Lagarde was far from being a universalist. Indeed, he was intensely chauvinistic and an early, rhetorically violent architect of a new German prometheanism.[40] For him, the genius of Jesus was the same as the genius of the Germans themselves. Jesus was similar to Copernicus; the Germans were also a Copernicus-like people, filled with intellectual independence and a sense of profound individuality and mystical freedom. Jesus overcame Judaism: the Germans must overcome the evils of liberalism and experience their own great hour of national rebirth and transfiguration. No "Russian coachman in a French harness" will flog the authentic, reborn Germany of the future with "Jewish whips"![41] This Germany-to-come will have its own specially constructed national faith rather than Christianity, an inauthentic and largely Jewish concoction that Paul, not Jesus had inflicted on the west. In spite of this angry denunciation, however, Lagarde never fully severed the umbilical cord that bound him to his Christian past. He still retained strong religious feelings, and his dream of a national *Wiedergeburt* owed a great deal to the romantic and pietistic currents that surrounded his Protestant youth (his family was acquainted with Schleiermacher), although it cannot be explained solely in these terms. In that sense, his anti-Christian religion of the future was the malformed offspring of Protestantism itself.

NATIONALISM CUM RACISM

Lagarde was an extreme Fichtean: a supernationalist but, in the technical sense at least, not a racist. Interestingly, he repudiated the new doctrines of race that German admirers of Gobineau, notably the Wagner circle, were starting to circulate in Wilhelmine Germany as both crude and scientifically worthless.[42] In spite of Lagarde's disapproval, however, it was only a matter of time – and not very much time – before German nationalism of the Fichtean-Lagardian variety would attach itself to this latest intellectual fad. Richard Wagner, the great composer and friend of Gobineau's, had poured his Germanic feelings and racial convictions into his music without restraint.[43] More significantly, however, Wagner's half-English son-in-law

Houston Stewart Chamberlain (1855–1927) composed what, in Germany at least, was destined to become the most influential racist writing after Gobineau's *Essai*. This was his quasi-philosophical composition *Die Grundlagen des XIX Jahrhunderts (The Foundations of the Nineteenth Century)* – a work that went into ten editions following its initial publication in 1899 and earned for its author the personal esteem of Wilhelm II. Chamberlain, the emperor declared, had charted the "salvation of the Germans" and thus the "salvation of mankind."[44] Not only did his *Foundations* provide contemporary German nationalism with an elaborate racial ideology, but his theories (Chamberlain was hailed in certain circles as the greatest German philosopher since Kant) prepared the Germans for the institutionalization of Aryan dogmas in the future Third Reich. At last, the Aryan myth came into its own on German soil; the Aryans and Teutons were firmly joined and those modern Germans who sought their collective *alter ego* in the lost, dim world of pre-Christian Germany could feel that they had truly found themselves. It was Chamberlain who, in Rousseauistic fashion, had supplied them with their "noble savage."

Not surprisingly, the new noble savage was everything that the decadent Europeans were not, in the same fashion that Tacitus's Germans were everything that his Roman contemporaries were not, although Tacitus, unlike Chamberlain, did not think in racial categories. Specifically, the Aryan-Teuton was the perfect contrast to the Semite, who was the bearer of all the unhealthy traits that had swept into Europe like an evil plague, particularly the spirit of materialism, which, in the eyes of the romantics (as well as the socialists), was the basis of capitalism. Jesus, the great Aryan – the "probability that Christ was no Jew, that He had not a drop of genuinely Jewish blood in his veins, is so great that it is almost a certainty"[45], – whose coming heralded the "morning of a new day,"[46] would cure society of its Semitic sickness by overcoming the materialists (i.e., capitalists) as he had once overcome the Pharisees, for capitalism was the modern Pharisaism.

A spurious Hegelian element in Chamberlain's thought can be easily detected. Judaism or Pharisaism (thesis) gave rise to Jesus (antithesis) in its bosom, but Jesus negated Judaism to produce Christianity (synthesis). A Galilean rather than a Jew, according to Chamberlain, and therefore the descendant of Aryan colonists in ancient Galilee, the founder of Christianity was raised in the religious ethos of Judaism, but, as a consequence of his racial distinctiveness, became its opposite pole. In contrast to Jewish formalism, rationalism, and legalism, Jesus brought a profound inner freedom, spiritual intuition, and religious emancipation. Against Jewish dreariness and incapacity for art, science, and philosophy, Jesus, "the richest mind that ever lived," produced a new creative vision of humanity.[47] Against Jewish utilitarianism, Jesus, "the religious genius of mankind," exalted a set of lofty values and a noble conception of deity.[48] No wonder the Jews crucified him: he had planted the "flag of idealism" on the soil of their "obstinate materialism," negating Judaism at its core.[49] Jesus was the supreme hero-genius of history whose transcendent originality made him the supreme symbol of the Aryan race, for virtue, intelligence, and creativity are properties of Aryan blood alone. Christianity, by which Chamberlain meant Protestant Christianity, was the natural religion of Aryan-Teutonic man. When Albert Réville, a French professor of comparative religion, dismissed the Aryan descent of Jesus as an idle question, Chamberlain was indignant at such obscurantist medievalism, believing that no modern mind could conceivably regard Jesus as a Jew.[50]

But Chamberlain was hardly a new Kant or Hegel. His racism was borrowed largely from Gobineau, his German supernationalism from Wagner and Lagarde, his biology from Darwin and the Darwinists, his anthropology from the French anthropologist Georges Vacher de Lapouge and others, his pseudo-mysticism from the neo-Kantians, and his views of Jews and Judaism from ages of cultural prejudice, both pre-Christian and Christian. Apion of Alexandria had long ago accused the Jews of lack of creativity,[51] and classical Christianity had long reiterated the theme that Judaism was a pernicious and materialistic legalism.[52] Christ as the abjurer of Pharisaism was an old idea, at least as old as Matthew's Gospel.[53] In spite of its serious failings, however, the Christian tradition (except Marcion) was usually careful to connect Jesus with the Hebrew scriptures and therefore to the people of Israel, whereas Germanic writers such as Lagarde and Chamberlain sundered all possible ties between Jesus and his Jewish roots. What genius requires any real explanation beyond himself? Not Copernicus, not Jesus. It was this godlike Jesus who could not be Jewish, only German or Aryan, for the Aryan spirit was also godlike. More and more, the Aryan Christ became a synonym for the essential divinity of Aryan man. Increasingly, as Bastide showed, the Aryanization of Christ required his transformation in accordance with the logic of colour symbolism [chapter I]: "It was necessary that this man ... be as far removed as possible from everything that would suggest darkness or blackness (e.g., Semitism), even indirectly: His hair and beard were given the color of sunshine, the brightness of the light above, while his eyes retained the color of the sky from which he descended and to which he returned."[54]

The twentieth century saw the Germanic Christ in full array. Chamberlain's imitators refined the Aryan identity of Jesus to their heart's content. Otto Weininger, a disturbed young Jewish admirer of Chamberlain, decided that Jesus was a Jew who had become an Aryan – a metemorphosis that Weininger sought to emulate.[55] Artur Dinter, a Nazi novelist, transformed Jesus into a Siegfried-type hero of Germanic mythology, replete with warrior qualities.[56] Others, including some of Lagarde's disciples, added Jesus to their pantheons of German and pseudo-Indian race gods.[57] Chamberlain, while far removed from orthodox Christianity, still spoke, albeit inconsistently, of the higher moral power of the cross, but later Aryanizers, taking their cue from another ex-Christian, Friedrich Nietzsche, increasingly regarded such moral feelings as forgiveness, love, and compassion as totally erroneous. Here, as Uriel Tal has pointed our, a deeper polemic against religion itself, especially in its biblical Christian form, was working its way into racist theory:

The principle of "Dionysus versus the Crucified One" (passion and not martyrdom) that was preached by Nietzsche, the rejection of religion as a corrosive historic force that perverted, poisoned, and debased man's natural instincts, the attack upon Christianity as the religion of the poor, the weak, and the disinherited and their hypocritical ideal of selflessness, humility, renunciation, and sacrifice that seriously undermined all the vital forces tending to promote or elevate the life-enhancing qualities of pride, courage, fortitude, and vital spontaneity all nourished racial anti-Semitism and endowed it with a non-Christian or anti-Christian significance.[58]

Nietzsche, in spite of these sentiments, was neither a racist nor an antisemite; nor did he think of Jesus as an Aryan. The salient fact about Jesus, as far as he was concerned, was not that Jesus was not Jewish, but that he was. Jesus, the "holy anarchist," who had stirred up the Jewish rabble to oppose the ruling classes of his own society, was actually a kind of religious fool, a Jewish political criminal, an "idiot" (Nietzsche had Dostoevski's famous character in mind).[59] For Nietzsche, only Ernest Renan, the author of the best-selling *Vie de Jésus* (1863), "that buffoon *in psychologicis,*' could have applied the two "most inapplicable concepts possible" to Jesus: the concept of the hero and the concept of the genius. "To make a *hero* of Jesus! – And what a worse misunderstanding is the word 'genius'!"[60] All the hero and genius christologies of the day were no more than facile expressions of German self-glorification, as exemplified, for example, by Nietzsche's own brother-in-law, the obnoxious Bernhard Förster, who saw himself as an apostle of the Aryan Christ even before

Chamberlain.[62] It was ironic, although not surprising, that the Dionysian aspects of Nietzsche's philosophy of existence – the life-enhancing qualities of pride, courage, fortitude, and vital spontaneity – became the ingredients of an ideology that he himself regarded as a painful symptom of the German disease. The philosopher's attack on Judaism and Jewish morality in *The Genealogy of Morals* gravely weakened his attempt to disparage the antisemitic movement that was gaining momentum in imperial Germany.

The contradictions inherent in a racialized Christianity could not be concealed indefinitely. An Aryan Christ was bound sooner or later to tear himself away from the pages of the New Testament, leaving his modern disciples in a state of confusion. Thus the "German Christians" of the Third Reich attempted in the same breath to profess "some knowledge" of Christian compassion toward the helpless as well as a "heroic piety" along Aryan lines.[62] Walter Grundmann, for example, a well-qualified biblical scholar and a distinguished contributor to Kittel's *Wörterbuch*, poured his energies into a futile effort to prove the Aryan descent of Jesus in order to eradicate all semblances of the hated Judaism from German Christianity.[63] Needless to say, his work was sponsored by the National Socialist regime. That some Germans simply abandoned Christianity altogether in favour of overt neo-paganism is scarcely surprising. They were at least more consistent than the German Christian theologians who maintained that the church should take "concrete form" in the National Socialist ethos in order to prevent its collapse into paganism.[64] But the new order and its ideology could not be Christianized any more than Christianity could be paganized and still remain Christianity. Nevertheless, the German Christians in both church and state managed to unite around the august figure of the Aryan Christ manufactured in their image. Jesus, stripped of his Jewishness, clothed in Aryan dress, and elevated to the status of a white German tribal deity, was the perfect religious symbol of a racist church in a totalitarian state.

GERMAN SACRED HISTORY

In 1897, two illustrious Germans, both romantic nationalists, warned the public against the "Jewish danger" in German society and, in effect, legitimized the antisemitic agitation already present in the politics of the Reich. One was the eminent historian Heinrich von Treitschke, who coined the memorable and deadly phrase, "The Jews are our misfortune."[65] The other was Adolf Stöcker, the emperor's court preacher, who, in order to attract supporters to his floundering Christian Social Workers' Party, decried Jewish power in the state.[66]

These ominous warnings coincided, paradoxically, with a movement to provide Germany with a new Christian identity as a consequence of Prince von Bismarck's *Kulturkampf* (1871–1887) or campaign against the independence of the German churches, especially Roman Catholicism.[67] The new "Christian" state, which was inspired largely by Lutheran ideas, was Christian only in an ideological sense. It signified the victory of a romantic nationalism whose *völkisch* protagonists strongly disliked the current political system because of its constitutional and parliamentary character. Jews, having found civil emancipation a difficult struggle because of its French egalitarian associations, depended for their security on constitutional rights; in the organic *Volk* of the neo-romantics, they were outsiders by definition. It was this subtle shift from liberalism to reaction, together with the social tensions of the era, that promoted the rise of political antisemitism in Germany as a means of uniting an insecure and still somewhat fragmented society. (Bismarck's policies, in fact, were a mask for the internal weaknesses of the Reich itself.) In this fashion, as in France during the same period, race doctrines gained a foothold in conservative circles, including religious ones.

Not all of the romantic nationalists were also racists, at least not at first. Stöcker himself actively resisted the new breed of racial antisemite personified by such men as Förster, Wilhelm Marr, Theodor Fritsch, and Eugen Dühring. His own hostility to Jews and Judaism was the product of Christian theology as well as *völkisch* romanticism. Hence, as a somewhat old-fashioned Christian, he rejected the racist thesis that Jesus was an Aryan rather than a Semite, and regarded its supporters as guilty of the "height of folly."[68] He advanced, however, the equally pernicious thesis that Germany was a holy nation, the true Israel, and that German Christians, not Christians in general, were the elect people of God in the modern world.[69] This political theology was destined to play a decisive role in the racialization of German Protestant Christianity during the Third Reich, but its first appearance was in the Second Reich. After Bismarck subjected the churches to greater civil control (largely, incidentally, by utilizing Luther's doctrine of Christian subservience to temporal rulers),[70] causing German nationalism to become "imbued with Lutheran symbols," the nation itself became the body of Christ in the eyes of many Lutherans.[71] If Germany was the true Israel, then German history was sacred history and the Germans alone were worthy to establish a Reich that would renew the great "tradition of the Carolingian Empire."[72] The Jews, on the other hand, were a false Israel, as they were in the eyes of early Christians once the church had expelled them from the sphere of God's grace; their history had ceased to be sacred history, and hence they dwelt in the shadows as enemies of the true Israel whose "Christian *Volk*-consciousness" they constantly sought to destroy.[73] Germany, holy Germany, was surely the medium of God's ineffable presence in the modern world. "Gott mit uns" was a Protestant as well as an imperial motto, the expression of German religious, political, and ethnic singlemindedness, or the numinous unity of altar, throne, and *Volk*.[74] What closer synthesis could possibly have united the Christian faith and the German soul? Even Fichte would have marvelled.

But there was a price to be paid for casting the fortunes of a modern power in such unself-critical and wholly self-centred terms: if these fortunes failed, a monumental crisis of faith was likely to ensue. The elect Germans, having plunged into a war in 1914 in a state of moral and religious euphoria, suffered a defeat they certainly did not expect and could scarcely believe when it occurred. It was difficult to see what the proud assertion "Gott mit uns" – the theme of countless wartime sermons – could mean after such a defeat. "With God for king and fatherland, for emperor and empire, for honour and freedom. The old God still lives. The Lord is nevermore separated from our people."[75] Who could reconcile these glowing words with the catastrophe of 1918, who could harmonize history with theology and theology with history? How, wondered Emanuel Hirsch, an eminent Lutheran theologian, can Christians regard the historical process as meaningful in the wake of Germany's downfall? The disaster visited on the heads of a "world people, a noble people, perhaps the most flourishing and best of all," exposed the "riddle of human history" and the "great conscientious issue of the life of the human community."[76] God, the Lord of history, allowed the war to end as it did largely, Hirsch decided, because the ecstatic sacrificial spirit with which Germany had entered the struggle, making those August days of 1914 so memorable and so beautiful, had sputtered out as the war advanced: the nation had betrayed itself, and, like Israel of old, had to suffer divine rebuke for this betrayal.[77] Its humiliation, however, could not long endure. The resurrection of holy Germany, together with the renewal of its innermost and deepest religious faith, was both a burning need and, in light of the scriptures, a providential certainty.

First, however, theology had to find a political nexus. The anti-historical theology of the contemporary dialectical theologians such as Karl Barth with its *deus absconditus* was anathema to the nationalistic theologians.[78] God must say "yes" and not "no" to history, especially to German history. Hirsch, wrestling with the spiritual meaning of Germany's defeat as Paul had once wrestled with the spiritual meaning of Israel's rejection of Christ, appealed to Fichte. Not only Fichte's mystical Germanism but also his idealistic belief in an essential relationship between the human consciousness and the divine consciousness, as opposed to all forms of scepticism and positivism, became the basis of his thought.[79] Naturally, this excluded the theological positivism of Barth and his followers. Hirsch, however, wedded his own qualified Kantian-Fichtean idealism to a Kierkegaardian awareness of the crucial importance of the present moment as a moment of decision in which the individual decides for or against an "absolute relationship to the Absolute."[80] The present moment is the historic moment, and the Absolute (God) is always present in the historic moment, even if the divine presence appears under imperfect finite forms. Consequently, sound theology must be historical theology, arising out of the free inner response of the religious conscience to the current situation and its spiritual demands, for all truth is ultimately the truth of conscience, and personal conscience is ultimately grounded in God. In the eyes of the intensely nationalistic Hirsch, the situation calling for spiritual decision was the fifteen years between 1918 and 1933, the period of exile and suffering endured by the German-Israelites until the new Moses showed them the way back to the promised land.[81]

It was the 1933 revolution, that "great holy storm of present-day *Volk*-happenings" ("*grossen heiligen Sturm gegenwärtigen Volkgeschehens*"),[82] or, as another Lutheran theologian, Karl Heim, described it, that wonderful moment when "for the first time in the towns of Germany all classes of people walked through the streets together in procession – peasants, tailors, and bakers, side by side with clergy and professors,"[83] which brought matters to a head. Here, the still small voice of the Lord of history seemed to address the Germans, demanding an either/or response. Hirsch himself apparently never doubted that the God of this rapturous occasion and the God of Christianity were the same. Faith discerned a transcendent presence in the political miracle of the National Socialist triumph, and the fact that, as Helmut Thielicke later declared, the self-anointed messiah of the movement draped himself deliberately in the "luminous robes" of an angel assisted this vision – robes that carefully concealed the devil's "cloven hoof."[84]

Like France following a similar national catastrophe in 1870, Germany after 1918 was a traumatized society: a once radiant emperor had tumbled from his throne, bringing down with him the imperial system itself. Although the Weimar Republic had been welcomed by the classes that had turned against the Kaiser and arranged his overthrow, it was fragile from the beginning, in part because it was conceived in the wake of a national humiliation that could be forgotten neither quickly nor easily. When the woes of financial collapse and mass unemployment descended on the nation in the post-war era, the political structures established to replace the vanished Reich were undermined further. Moreover, there were deeper causes of the destabilization of German democracy. "What was peculiar to Weimar Germany was ... the passionate intensity of the emotional revulsion against the machine age and mass society, and the profound need to escape from a realistic analysis of social alternatives into the dream of a national and spiritual rebirth."[85] Conservative German Protestants shared a popular, if not universal, disdain for the Republic as an illegitimate and decadent institution imposed on a defeated and perhaps betrayed Germany by her alien foes. Vengeful and xenophobic feelings increased. A fresh menace arose in the east in the form of Russian Bolshevism, making the German political and social situation more precarious than ever. Was a second revolution impending?

The deadly winds of racism and antisemitism began to blow, threatening the house of cards in Berlin that sheltered the nation's democratic aspirations. With the Aryan myth as their animating force, they promised national and racial revitalization. Antisemitism had entered German politics with the election of Otto Böckel in 1887 and Herman Ahlwardt in 1892 to the old Reichstag on antisemitic platforms; the stage was now set for its return. Any politician or political movement that truly understood the *Zeitgeist* and was willing to lean as the winds blew had an auspicious future. When, through intrigue and luck, Hitler finally made himself the ruler of Germany, he was hailed with enormous enthusiasm by many Germans, including many Christians. The new leader's "carefully guarded image ... [as] an upholder of religion and the churches and a crusading knight against bolshevism, at once a defender of Germany's honor and the regenerator of the German nation,"[86] served him in good stead. Romantic and nationalistic Protestant theologians, with their fixations concerning the German soul, were not unaffected by these winds; without hesitation, and with few second thoughts, they stepped into the dark and fateful waters of racism.

THE RACIST CAPTIVITY OF THE
GERMAN CHRISTIAN THEOLOGIANS

This tragedy was assisted by more than the narcissistic allure and seductive power of the Aryan myth. The contemporary revival of Luther studies had revived Luther's social and political doctrines, i.e., the so-called "orders of creation" (*Theologie der Schöpfungsordnungen*). These orders or ordinances – marriage, church, and state

– were believe to be rooted in the word of God, making them the foundation of all true order in the world. In classical Lutheranism, God's word, by imposing a definitive and hallowed structure on a sinful human community, saves it from chaos and moral confusion. The orders of creation, however, could be interpreted in various ways depending on the bias of the interpreter and the concerns of society at a given time. Luther himself, fearful of social anarchy during an age of serious unrest – the peasants' insurrection – had emphasised the authority of the princely rulers as God's appointees who were to be disobeyed only at one's religious peril. The state was a mighty bulwark against evil, and earthly power was the sword of God's left hand, although Luther had no illusions concerning the character of princes who, more often than not, were the "biggest fools or the worst scoundrels on earth," the wise prince being "a mighty rare bird."[87] While this theory sanctioned authoritarianism, it had no connection with racism which, like nationalism, did not exist in Luther's day (if we except the special case of sixteenth-century Spain). In the modern Luther revival, however, a heavy infusion of German romanticism altered the original sense of Luther's ideas. The nation itself rather than the political apparatus of the nation, was held by some of the neo-Lutherans to be the real order of creation, thereby recasting Luther's doctrine in a racist mould. Popular feeling, not for the first time in Christian history, carried official theology toward a dangerous destination whose nature would soon become obvious.

This new interpretation of Luther occurred at the worst possible moment in modern Germany. A political crisis was brewing, and the nature of political authority was a major issue. Protestant theology was also in the throes of a crisis not unrelated to the political crisis. Nationalistic theologians were equally dissatisfied with the old religious liberalism, the more recent Barthian dialectical theology, and an "unbridled heathen volkish ideology" that conceded nothing to Christianity and everything to the German soul.[88] The last of these options greatly alarmed those churchmen who, in spite of their romantic nationalism, still saw themselves essentially as the sons of the Reformation and the custodians of its traditions. For example, Paul Althaus, who did as much as anyone to promote the theology of the orders of creation (Richard Gutteridge describes him as the principal architect),[89] tried to fend off this danger. "We do not want a Germanic church, but a German church, which not only preaches among its own *Volk* but lives historically through them. We do not want a *völkisch* church which distorts and restricts law and gospel in terms of a *völkisch* worldview; but we want a peoples' church (*Volkkirche*) which enters with love into the life of its *Volk* and which strives for an ever new Germanization and contemporary realization of its message."[90] The enemy that Althaus had in mind was primarily Jakob Wilhelm Hauer and his new Germanic religion with its peculiar mixture of old German mythology, Indian monism, and cyclical time.[91] Hauer, a former missionary to India and a committed racist, undoubtedly represented a serious threat to German Protestantism. But, as a defender of the dominant tradition, Althaus was too thoroughly captivated by the idea of a Germanic spirit to argue effectively against nationalist onslaughts. Theologians who, in Wolfgang Tilgner's words, idealized the *Volk* as an "eternal myth" and a "metaphysical order of creation," were in a weak position to criticize ex-Christians such as Hauer who had deserted the church.[92] In the final analysis, the Aryan Christ of the German Christians and the deified Aryan of Hauer, Rosenberg, and Günther were part of the same continuum: the former was easily dissolved into the latter.

A comparison of the varying interpretations of Luther's orders among the theologians of the *Theologie der Schöpfungsordnungen* school reveals how easy it was to move from orthodox Christianity to unorthodox racism once the racist virus had entered the Christian bloodstream. To Emil Brunner, a non-German and non-Lutheran associated with the counter-movement of dialectical theology but nevertheless attracted to certain Lutheran ideas, the family rather than the state was the basic order from which the other orders were derived. While Brunner believed that Christians should be grateful that they belonged to nations, since nationhood is part of God's calling, he repudiated the notion that the nation-state should be considered "*the* form of life willed by God" because nations (i.e., peoples) are always appearing and disappearing in history, and lack genuine integrity.[93] To be sure, the state is a necessary institution, and nationhood – a sense of collective identity or peoplehood (*Volkstum*) – is the logical foundation of the state, but to regard the latter as the "aggregate of all human life" is to fall under a terrible delusion which leads directly to totalitarianism, the dominant sickness of the twentieth century.[94]

Friedrich Gogarten, a German Lutheran with strong nationalistic sympathies, saw the matter differently. The state rather than the family was the fundamental order, including and transcending the other orders because it alone was grounded in a profound recognition of the awful peril posed by evil in each instant of life; a peril that Christian ethics must never forget if it is to argue meaningfully about the nature of human society. "The polis or the state is that order by means of which man seeks to secure himself against chaos and the destructive powers which menace his existence in the world, and against the powers of destruction which originate in his own peculiar being."[95] On the very eve of the National Socialist revolution, Gogarten, in a "complex and disturbing book," uttered a "somber endorsement of the grandeur of the state as the instrument of God to restrain evil."[96] The irony of his timing – he welcomed the demise of the "individualistic" and "anarchistic" Weimar Republic as presumably too weak to protect Germany against the powers of darkness[97] – requires no comment. What does require comment is the extent to which fear of individualism and anarchy can result in an excessive reliance on aggregates with, as Martin Buber once remarked in a critique of Gogarten, a consequent diminishing of personal ethical responsibility.[98] Gogarten's vision was fixed on the political aggregate in the classical Lutheran sense, but he was sufficiently influenced by German romanticism to speak of the *Volk* as the deeper basis of human community and social morality.[99] Once again, the influence of Fichte (about whom, incidentally, Gogarten had written his first book) was apparent: "But we go still deeper. However highly we wish to regard it, the state is always only external form and external law. Life itself, which needed this form and law in order to appear, arises out of another source. It arises out of the *Volk*. And this national life, this nationality and organ, is also that which gives to the state and to all political and social arrangements their value."[100] Gogarten did not press this Fichtean notion to racist conclusions. Rather than a biological organism (blood and race), he thought of the nation in personalistic (I-Thou) terms as a type of spiritual unity with a moral character of its own – the true bulwark against chaos.[101] With Gogarten, however, German Protestant theology was already teetering on the precipitous edge of racism.

Paul Althaus gave it a further push. To the Erlangen professor, the Fichtean definition of the nation as the "life-unity of men of a similar spiritual type" manifesting itself in language, thought, art, politics, and religion, was not only valid but a mark of God's creation.[102] *Volk* and *Volkstum*, consequently, are profound occasions for Christian thankfulness: "We see [God's] creative will in the Volkish differentiation of humanity."[103] For this reason, Althaus elaborated, "We love our *Volk*, and are pledged to stake our very lives for it, because it is indeed through God's ordinance our *Volk*."[104] One must protect what one loves – God requires no less – and this necessity raised deep apprehensions over the status of aliens in Germany's midst, i.e., the Jews, whose threatening presence seemed to endanger God's sacred order. On this subject, however, Althaus was curiously ambivalent. Neither a racist nor an antisemite, at least in his own opinion, he apparently believed that the best way to deal with the secular ideologies of racism and antisemitism was to draw their sting by Christianizing their premises. Racial integrity was presented as sound theology and the Jews were portrayed as a racial menace to the German nation. As if, however, disturbed by the hazards inherent in these concessions to the popular *Zeitgeist*, Althaus sought to neutralize them by reminding his Christian readers that the Jewish presence in Germany also possessed "divine significance" as an "indication of the limits and relativity of volkish separation" and as a token of the more universal Kingdom of God.[105] To this degree the nationalist was also a universalist.

Brunner described Althaus's position correctly as a "half-way house" between romanticism and the Reformation.[106] Unlike the more radical German Christians, Althaus shrank from the full implications of what, in his own words, was deemed the "German hour of the church."[107] However sacred the *Volk* as God's creation, salvation came through Christ and not through the orders, nor should the German *Volk* be confused with the Hebrew *Volk*, or German history with biblical sacred history. The Hebrews, and the Hebrews alone, had received a once-and-for-all revelation from God, and their scriptures (the Old Testament) remained inviolable and irreplaceable.[108] For Lutherans to think otherwise would mean a betrayal of Luther, who, in spite of everything, was always the conscious centre of Althaus's theological loyalties and the anchor which saved him from drifting too far toward the shoals of total racism. Yet the scope for racializing the word of God within the broad frame of Lutheran orthodoxy itself was obviously considerable.

Emanuel Hirsch was even more influenced by racist ideas. With Fichte as his mentor, this immensely gifted theologian argued that the state was merely a matrix for the *Volk*, the true order of creation whose unfolding life had religious and revelatory meaning. History, the realm of God's lordship, is animated by the divine presence, and the *Volk*, as the "hidden sovereign of the state," is the medium of this presence.[109] To seek God, therefore, means to turn toward the *Volk* as the concrete manifestation of the Creator's will which requires unconditional obedience and discipleship from the Christian. The state exists for the sake of the *Volk*, as the "guarantor" of its freedom; should it inhibit this freedom (as did the ill-fated Weimar Republic), it can be overthrown. True obedience has a larger focus: "Fidelity to the Lord becomes the sanctification of fidelity to the blood and the people or nation."[110] Hirsch, perhaps influenced by the nationalistic historian Heinrich von Treitschke and his famous lectures on German history, seems to have regarded even war as part of the order of creation.[111] While such sentiments could have been uttered with impunity during the nineteenth century, the age of Social Darwinism, after 1914 only a total refusal to accept reality could have allowed anyone to think of warfare as morally invigorating.

Hirsch, without disavowing his Lutheran heritage, had moved far from Luther's own position, in spite of the latter's support for the German nobility during the civil strife of the sixteenth century. For Hirsch, the invocation of blood was fraught with racial significance, disclosing a fusion of racism and romanticism at the core of Protestant piety. Blood is an ancient metaphor for the "essence of man, the principle of life," intimately linked by the Greeks to the "concept of human generation."[112] Consequently, it has a spiritual as well as a biological connotation, joining the mystery of our invisible nature to the mystery of our fleshly origins. This double meaning was constantly visible in the musings of the racists, who never wearied of detecting a correspondence between the outer and inner or physical and mental (and spiritual) traits of the various races: a beautiful – according to Aryan standards – body signified a superior intellect and a noble soul, whereas an ugly body signified the reverse. The materialistic foundations of this Gobinist belief emerged with special clarity in Chamberlain, for whom the laws of race and blood were primary and the *fons et origo* of all mental qualities.[113] When Hirsch attached spiritual health to racial determination, he exposed the extent to which the secular and anti-biblical ideas of the racist philosophers had seeped into his theology:

All human creating and shaping is limited and bounded by the natural character that we bring into life with us. If the blood is ruined, so also the spirit dies, for the spirit of nations and men arises out of the blood. Only the excessive pride of an intellectual generation that knew no limit to human ability in the mystery of our given creatureliness was able to forget it, causing infinite damage with its forgetfulness. The bloodbond of our nation was in ruin. If another fifty years had unfolded, the bearers of good, old and pure German blood (the leading classes of our nation) would have sunk into a minority. With its belief in creation, the church now has the possibility of keeping sacred the mystery of that power and character given with the blood.[114]

It was not Hirsch's intention to submerge Christianity in a sea of paganism. Instead, while endorsing the National Socialist revolution, he sought its Christianization in order to prevent a pagan triumph in post-Weimar Germany. But Pandora's box had been opened, and German Protestantism was now haunted by racist spectres. Their influence was increased by other intellectual currents, notably neo-Kantianism with its mystical Germanic distortions. Not all the neo-Kantians – or even all of Fichte's admirers – were intoxicated by race doctrines; any such suggestion would be a gross overstatement. The young Martin Buber, as a *fin de siècle* prophet of Jewish rejuvenation, had conceived of a Jewish *Volk* exemplified by the Hasidim,[115] and the young Paul Tillich had dreamed of the rejuvenation of German society after World War I through a religious socialism inspired by a rediscovery of the transcendent dimensions of life.[116] (Hirsch, as an early friend of Tillich, employed some of the latter's ideas, especially the concept of *kairos,* for his own quite different political agenda – a situation that led to a bitter rupture between the two theologians after Tillich's departure for the United States.)[117]

With Hirsch, the racist seeds embedded in the German idealistic tradition from its early days came to full blossom, despite his Christian faith. Not for the first time in Christian history, a morally earnest man became an apostle of evil principles. What was true of Hirsch was true of many others as well: swept away by the passions of the time, they found it surprisingly easy to accept racist ideas. All the neo-Lutheran theologians of the *Theologie der Schöpfungsordnungen* school had to do was to decide that, according to the divine decree, humanity-in-general did not exist, only nations and races-in-partic-ular.[118] Regrettably, in his post-World War II book *Ethos und Evangelium,* the elderly and unrepentant Hirsch, still clung to his Fichtean assumptions.[119]

THE ARYAN LAWS (1933–35)

The hour of trial for German Protestantism arrived when the National Socialist regime, almost immediately following its ascent to power, imposed laws designed to exclude non-Aryans from public office. Racial dreams could now be incarnated as political reality, and the German Christian faction lost no time in calling for Aryanization in the church as well as the state, together with the implementation of the "leadership principle." "It is more important that a theological student should know something about eugenics, heredity, and science than that he should have his head stuffed with the names and dates of Jewish kings."[120] These cries coincided with the onslaught of organized boycotts against Jewish businesses in the Reich: an omen of things worse to come. Confronted with the new situation, the Protestant leadership responded in a variety of ways. For example, the young Reformation Movement (*Jungreformatorische Bewegung*) of Martin Niemoller, Walter Künneth, and Hans Lilje protested on

Christian grounds against any attempt to exclude non-Aryans from full participation in the church; in the same breath, however, they affirmed their political loyalty to the state.

During the ensuing debate, two theological faculties, Marburg and Erlangen, were consulted for their collective wisdom. The Marburg theologians, including Rudolf Bultmann, opposed the introduction of racial categories into the church, but the Erlangen theologians (Paul Althaus and Werner Elert) argued that the visible organization of the Christian community should correspond to the historical and *völkisch* divisions of the Christian world as well as to the universality of the gospel.[121] Unlike Roman Catholicism, which, although Althaus and Elert did not elaborate on this, represented in their minds a false and artificial (Latin) "universal" church order, Reformation Christianity appreciated the integrity of the *Volk* and heeded the Pauline teaching that every Christian should obey God within his particular calling (I Cor. 7:20).[122] If the *Volk* is one's calling, and if the *Volk* has a biological meaning, then any serious connection with the universal aspects of the gospel and the universal nature of the human community is instantly dissolved. The Jews, who might or might not be Germans – Althaus and Elert begged the question – were certainly not regarded as Germans by most of the German people, which was the important consideration. Indeed, in the context of contemporary Germany's "special biological-historical situation," the Jews were both an alien nationality and a menace whose presence called for a vigorous response.[123] In the struggle for national renewal, when the church was obliged to take seriously its duty as a national church, those who could not share in Germany's destiny should, following the new principles of exclusion adopted by the state, certainly not be mixed with Germans in Christian congregations through official or pastoral roles. In effect, Althaus and Elert sacralized the Aryan laws as a legitimate means of national self-defence against assimilated Jews.

As one might expect, the shadow of Luther, although distorted, was still in the background, especially his doctrine of the two realms with its dualistic distinction between the private and public aspects of life. Christian unity – all are one in Christ Jesus – was unassailable on the spiritual level; even the German Christians were forced to concede that much. Outwardly, however, this statement of faith did not apply. Racial divisions in the body of Christ were regarded both as natural and as consonant with the Creator's will. Consequently baptism, the sacrament of incorporation into Christ, had no bearing on the material form of the church; it was as irrelevant to the German

Christians as it had once been to the Spanish authors of the old anti-Jewish "purity of blook" restrictions in late medieval Spain. Althaus and Elert did not speak of an ineradicable Jewish proclivity toward infidelity and vice, but the concessions to popular antisemitism in the Erlangen document are obvious.

Nor were the Erlangen theologians isolated cases in Nazi Germany: other professors, notably Hans Müller, George Wobbermin, and Gerhard Kittel, followed suit.[124] The details of the controversy and the subsequent church struggle have been described by E.C. Helmreich and others.[125] While there was substantial opposition to the National Socialist attempt to remodel the evangelical churches along racial and authoritarian lines, few Protestants saw clearly the mortal danger in which German Christianity now stood. Even many of Hitler's enemies were infected by racism and antisemitism. Barth, who was not a German, certainly sensed the deeper peril, but Dietrich Bonhoeffer was almost alone at the time in discerning the true implications of the Aryan laws for the future of the church. Like Alonso de Cartegena before him, he defended the integrity of baptism as the great rite of Christian unity that in no wise can be robbed of its plain and simple meaning by racial arguments. Ironically, however, even the Protestant hero-martyr of the anti-Nazi resistance to the anti-Jewish and totalitarian policies of the Third Reich did not completely escape antisemitism. In attacking the German Christians, Bonhoeffer resorted to anti-Judaism himself by asserting that the church, if it adopted the Aryan laws, would be guilty of slipping into *Jewish* legalism.[126] Had he survived the war, he would surely have repented of this sentiment.

That a program of institutional racism could receive even a modicum of support from the custodians of Germany's Reformation heritage was a symptom of how far the disease had spread even prior to Hitler's coup. Piper did not exaggerate the importance of the "German movement" of the late eighteenth and nineteenth centuries as a prelude to the nationalistic aberrations of the Third Reich.[127] Its influence was such that even the greatest of scholars were affected: Karl Holl, for example, in his otherwise profound discussion of the cultural significance of the Reformation, commented that imperialism "could never possess the German people" because, unlike the English, they were too fearful of its spiritual consequences.[128] Such odd remarks were legion in German scholarship, especially biblical scholarship where, as we have seen, the new Germanism finally created a Germanic Jesus after its own dark image. Slowly and insidiously the

Reformation churches were infected by a nationalistic and racist virus that Luther, for all his faults and weaknesses, would never have countenanced. The mighty word of God had become a racist word of blood, *Volk,* and soil, whose ethic of struggle, violence, and death would find its consummation in Hitler's Final Solution.

CHAPTER THREE

The Latin Christ

Although he can hardly be blamed, Tacitus was the godparent of French as well as German racism. The Roman historian's "bizarre conception" of the Germans as a people "smitten with liberty, austere, sober, moral, but courageous and warlike" was introduced into French political literature by Francis Hotman, a great Calvinist critic of royal tyranny during the late sixteenth century.[1] No more a racist than Tacitus, Hotman only wished to defend the libertarian foundations of the French political system against the encroachments of an absolutistic monarchy obsessed with the "divine right of kings." Hence he contended in his *Franco-Gallia* (1573) that France was formed at the end of the period of Roman power by a voluntary association of Frankish (i.e., German) and Gallic tribesmen on the basis of tribal democracy and elective kingship. "This is clearly the form of rule that our Gauls had before they were subjected to the power of the Romans," Hotman declared, "since the people, as Caesar says, had no less dominion and power over the king than the king over the people. But it is likely that our Franks derived this form of constitution not from the Gauls but from their fellow Germans, of whom Tacitus … writes: 'The power of their kings was not unlimited and free.'"[2] Despite the lack of any suggestion of Frankish conquest or racial superiority in *Franco-Gallia*, this interpretation of the origins of the nation was later twisted in order to promote both these ideas, thereby justifying class and race distinctions in French society after Hotman's day. It was, with modifications, crucial to Count Gobineau.

Prior to the eighteenth-century revolution, however, another French aristocrat, Count de Boulainvilliers (whose title, incidentally, unlike Gobineau's, was not spurious), sundered the French into two races: the "Franks," or the racial descendants of the supposed German conquerors of old Gaul, – the current nobility – and the "Gauls," or the racial descendants of the conquered Romans and Celts, i.e., the middle and lower classes.[3] This political myth served as a powerful rationale for aristocratic ascendancy, although, by the time the revolution occurred, the nobility had lost its power, if not its status, in the nation.

As Alexis de Tocqueville observed in his famous study of the old regime, pre-revolutionary France was a house deeply divided, with noble and bourgeois not merely rivals but enemies.[4] Unlike the English nobility, the French nobility had evolved from an "aristocracy" into a "caste": birth, and birth alone, determined its membership, producing a rigidity that forbade any crossing of class lines through intermarriage or promotion. Moreover, this social *rigor mortis* coincided with a remarkable gain of privilege under the later Bourbons, based, of course, on blood rather than merit. Already cut off by caste restrictions from social elevation, the bourgeoisie grew furious at the unmerited honours heaped on the undeserving upper classes, especially when the latter abandoned feudal *noblesse oblige* and any useful state function. Eventually the fury of the Third Estate overflowed into both the act of revolution and the reign of terror instigated by the Jacobins once they gained power. Not only the nobles, but the racial arguments of Boulainvilliers for their innate superiority, came to grief in the convulsions of 1789–95. Revolutionary ideologues, such as Abbé Emmanuel Joseph Sieyès, had only to invert the French political myth in order to discomfort their class foes. The anticipated victors were obviously the superior race. "In truth," Sieyès argued, "if one insists upon distinguishing between race and race, could not one reveal to our poor fellow-citizens the fact that being descended from the Gauls and Romans is worth at least as much as being descended from Sicambrians, Welch, and other savages out of the woods and marshes of old Germany?"[5] Perhaps it was Gallic rather than Frankish blood that was more reliable!

Those noble families that survived the guillotine became, as one might expect, deeply estranged from the new social order constructed out of the ashes of the old, leaving them primed for racist sentiments and ideas when the latter started to flourish during the nineteenth century. Such ideas allowed them to reinforce their caste identity. While Gobineau himself was not a genuine aristocrat, having adopted the title of a deceased uncle without proper authorization, he aspired to élitist status with the same hunger as the rest of his chosen caste. As the author of the first comprehensive account of the history of the world from a racial point of view, it was his contribution to sweep the older French political myth, derived from Hotman and Boulainvilliers as well as others, into the grander setting of the new

Aryan myth. There were, however, certain changes. Gobineau regarded Boulainvilliers as too simplistic, since the Germanic blood of the Frankish upper classes was not as pure as the earlier writer had imagined.[6] Unlike Hotman, moreover, the "father of racist ideology" thought of Germanic freedom as feudal privilege rather than democratic right. For Gobineau, the egalitarian revolution, hailed by the republicans as a *novus ordo saeculorum*, represented nothing less than the fall of France and the beginning of the end for the whole of Western Civilization. His pessimism was extreme.

THE FRENCH REVOLUTION

In observing that modern racism developed in conjunction with political symbols, Biddiss has also drawn attention to the element of social alienation embedded in Gobineau's philosophy.[7] Alienation (*alienatio*) has come to mean a sense of radical estrangement from the surrrounding social order that can result in a loss of personal selfhood or of personal self-esteem. Having suffered grief and loss, the victim of this deep spiritual disorder seeks both an explanation and redress, if not also a scapegoat. At the same time, an alienated person characteristically embarks on a guest for new structures of meaning – myths, symbols, ideas – in order to recover at least the illusion of health and security. While alienation can lead great writers and thinkers to profound insights into the complexities of human existence, it is potentially dangerous and can lead more ordinary individuals to extremism of thought and action.

This danger has been illustrated repeatedly since the beginning of the nineteenth century, when manifold economic, social, political, and cultural transformations overwhelmed Europe and altered the course of its history. The Industrial Revolution, for example, uprooted peasant families from the countryside and spawned an urban proletariat amid its "dark Satanic mills".[8] Capitalism, the financial catalyst of modern industrialization, seemed the archdemon of the age to those on both the left and the right of the political spectrum who dreamt of a less individualistic, less acquisitive, less unstable society, whether pre- or post-modern. If its critics are correct, from capitalism and its various works came a host of evils, notably "loneliness, frustation, hostility, insanity, crime":[9] in short, dehumanization on a scale never before experienced in history. Not only revolutionary but also reactionary writers were highly vociferous in their condemnation of industrial capitalism as having robbed men, women, and children of their legitimate human birthright.[10] To the romantic reactionaries especially, the most serious offence of the new social order was the manner in which it vitiated the deep, mysterious, and holy depths of life itself, especially communal life. Out of the social wilderness created by the economic upheavals of the industrial age, dissident voices clamoured in diverse ways. One was Karl Marx. Another was Richard Wagner, who savagely attacked the capitalistic curse through his operas.

Yet capitalism was not the only archdemon to be named by the voices of dissent: the French Revolution appeared in the same guise, at least to those unsympathetic to its political and philosophical principles. According to Eliade, the Aryan myth appealed to Europeans – not just Frenchmen – who were unable to accept the political results of 1789 and 1848.[11] Why were these revolutions so unsettling? Why did men such as Gobineau sink into a malaise so terrible that they could only recover from their spiritual exhaustion by attaching themselves to a new noble hero and primordial ancestor? As we saw in Chapter I, Biddiss has suggested that the rise of scepticism in the eighteenth century was related to the destabilization of accepted and treasured intellectual, religious, and social patterns. Thus the French Revolution, and the train of revolutions in its wake, signified more than simply a rearrangement of the political system of the day: it signified the collapse of an entire world-order, indeed, of a cosmology that the great majority of Europeans had regarded as inviolable. While old worlds must die in order that new worlds can be born, their dissolution, even when gradual, is always an unsettling experience for those who remain attached to former modes of thought. The downfall of familiar and beloved symbols threatens our sense of who and what we are. Feudalism was unjust, but the sacral kingdoms of the Christian Middle Ages at least supplied an identity in a hierarchical scheme of things for even the most lowly members of society. If the economic disturbances caused by industrialization were a major source of mass alienation in the modern era, the political disturbances unleashed by the age of revolution were equally potent as far as an important segment of the population was concerned. Biddiss is surely correct in believing that revolution in the political order had as much to do with the emergence of racism as revolution in the economic order had to do with the emergence of Marxism and other forms of radical socialism.[12]

Stemming from the explosion of 1789, therefore, a chain reaction was ignited that began to consume old regimes with their Christian foundations, making the subsequent period one of constant unrest as revolutionary and anti-revolutionary factions contended with each other. This uncertain and fluctuating situation accounted for the deep personal alienation felt by the losers in these struggles, usually the reactionaries. Moreover, as Edmund Burke once observed, the "vast, tremendous, unformed spectre" of remorseless violence that arose from the "tomb of the murdered monarchy in France" posed an unprecedented threat to all forms of established order in all countries, not merely to its immediate neighbours.[13] The Irish parliamentarian sensed that something altogether new, something more totalistic in its scope and titanic in its energy than any previous upheaval, had erupted from the depths: the throbbing passion of modern nationalism. Henceforth, the world would have no peace. Burke was also prophetic in another respect. In criticizing the fanatical determination of the French republicans to crush all classes of citizens into "one homogenous mass," leaving nothing between the people and the government, he predicted that, should monarchy ever return to France, it would return as the "most arbitrary power that ever appeared on earth."[14] With Napoleon, the first modern dictator, this prophecy was fulfilled, and, as we have already seen, Napoleonic imperialism was instrumental in the rise of alienation, nationalism, proto-racism, and latent aggression in Germany. In another sphere, the military and political tremors started by the French Revolution and by Napoleon had even more profound consequences. Shaken by the dramatic destruction of old historic institutions, many Christians, especially in England, concluded that the end of the world was at hand.[15] Their alienation from the present age produced a new crop of apocalyptic sects characterized by dire forebodings and (biblical) calculations of the end-time.

Gobineau himself, although born in 1816, wrote out of feelings of extreme alienation. Having identified his own fortunes with a caste that had been overthrown in 1789, he detested an age that had turned against his aristocratic (racial) lineage and values. In his estrangement, he consoled himself with sad reflections on the impending death of civilization, although there is sufficient narcissism in his pages to suggest that his own death was also the object – perhaps the true object – of his contemplation. The revolution of 1848, which marked the overthrow of the July monarchy of King Louis Philippe, prompted Gobineau's *Essai*, composed, incidentally, in Switzerland during the author's sojourn as a French legate (1849–54). Here, in the cradle of European democracy, he had the opportunity to observe its evils at close range, which, of course, he associated with the hated revolutionary tradition. Democracy for Gobineau meant mobocracy, and the mob meant that racial abyss found at the bottom of every society, but especially in France where degenerate elements were always poised to devour everything noble, precious, and beautiful. Metropolitan Paris in particular, with its racial miscegenation, was scarcely more than a giant cesspool swimming with uprooted men (*les déracinés*) ripe for violence and revolution: a perfect symbol of the modern social order.[16] To the jaded man-of-letters, the would-be aristocrat, these "deep stagnant waters" over which the fragile structure of civilization was suspended were steadily rising, and France – and Europe – would soon be submerged.[17] If race was the key to history, and if the modern city created by the Industrial Revolution was the paradigm of the future, there was little or nothing to be hoped for as far as Gobineau, the self-appointed physician of the social organism, was concerned.

Such sentiments on Gobineau's part were not mere affectations but reflect a discord that ran through every fibre of his being and coloured all of his perceptions. He was neither the first nor the last example of this kind of discord. In his seminal study of resentment (*ressentiment*) as a social phenomenon, Max Scheler cited Nietzsche's famous indictment of Tertullian, the church father of antiquity, for having portrayed the spectacle of pagan Romans burning in hell as one of the chief delights of his Christian heaven.[18] For Nietzsche, that ignoble desire made Tertullian's Christianity seem little more than a "continuous vengeance taken on the values of antiquity" – the sublimated hatred of the ex-pagan for the society he had abandoned.[19] Such are the cultural and ideological effects of repressed emotions. Despite the vast differences between Tertullian and Gobineau, it is possible to see the French writer in a similar light. Certainly the element of resentment is conspicuous in Gobineau's contempt for political democracy as a sign of decadence, and his racial ideas can be interpreted as a mode of vengeance on the values of modernity. Rome had disappointed Tertullian by not converting to Christianity; Europe disappointed Gobineau by turning against the glories of medieval civilization and the rule of the best.

As a Catholic in name only, Gobineau probably did not believe in hell and so could not have arranged for the egalitarians to burn in its flames, but he certainly thought that their world was headed for dissolution, and that he possessed the true faith. If western civilization perished, it would be because it had signed its own death warrant. As Mosse has pointed out, Gobineau effectively exposed his underlying feelings about his own age by projecting – no doubt unconsciously – all of the unsavoury traits of those segments of French society that he despised most, the bourgeoisie and the mob, onto the yellow and black races, the cotton and wool of the tapestry of human history. The self-serving materialistic oriental of the *Essai* was really an anti-capitalist's portrait of the money-grubbing French middle class, and the sensual, unintelligent, and violent negro was an aristocrat's portrait of the inhabitants of the Parisian backstreets who were ready for revolution at a moment's notice. The Aryan, on the other hand, was Gobineau's chosen class: the idealized blueblood of his romantic imagination who had been cheated of his rightful place in society by the rabble. In glorifying the noble Aryan, the silver and gold of the tapestry, the philosopher sought to cure his own profound unhappiness.

ARYAN AND SEMITE

Gobineau, in spite of his obvious prejudices, was not especially antisemitic, allowing the "secondary families" of the white race (i.e., the Semites, of whom the Jews were only a single branch) to add their silk to the cotton and wool of the lesser peoples. Silk, however, is less valuable than silver and gold; consequently, the Semites were less valuable than the Aryans, although, having white skins, of greater worth than the various species of yellow and black humanity. They were, in fact, really debased Aryans whose veins unfortunately contained a mixture of white and black blood as a result of historical circumstance.[21] Since, as we said in chapter one, white and black were polar opposites for the Europeans, to describe the Semites in this fashion was to take an implicit step in the direction of a new racial dualism that was destined to play an immense part in the subsequent evolution of European racism. A race myth required racial contrast and racial domination at its core, and, as Poliakov has emphasized, the Aryan myth, especially in the hands of its later popularizers, quickly acquired a dualistic character once it was applied to contemporary political issues in the European nations, notably the burning question of the nineteenth century – the emancipation of the Jews.[22]

To describe this development, Poliakov coined the term "racial Manichaeism" to describe a system in which two races are gradually transformed into antithetical symbols around which the conflicting elements in human existence are organized: goodness and evil, life and death, beauty and ugliness, creative and destructive energy, reason and emotion, youth and age, etc.[23] Such dualistic simplifications, including colour dualism, are both ancient and universal in the history of religion and culture and appear to be indigenous to human nature. Manichaeism is not the only example of a dualistic religion, and even non-dualistic religions such as popular Christianity reveal dualistic tendencies. In nineteenth-century Europe, Aryans and Semites, largely because of Western anti-Judaism/antisemitism, became the focus of this symbolic point-counterpoint. The Aryan was increasingly seen as the representation of the ideal white, upper- or upper-middle-class European while the Semite (Jew) came to represent the debased non-white, non-upper-or upper-middle-class European: the resident alien *par excellence.* The fact that Semites were as "white" as Frenchmen, Englishmen, or Germans, and as upper or upper-middle class in many instances, was entirely beside the point. Symbols need not correspond to surface reality. To understand the full significance of the Aryan myth during the racist era that began in the middle of the nineteenth century, it is necessary to examine this trend toward racial Manichaeism more closely.

By describing the Semites as impure Aryans whose blood was partially black, Gobineau not only succumbed to an ancient form of racial polarization, but also illustrated the extent to which the various racial antagonisms were interconnected on one level or another, despite the fact that the father of racist ideology and his many intellectual heirs never agreed among themselves as to the exact number of races and sub-races in the world. Contrast was the important consideration, and colour was the most potent mode of suggesting contrast. How could the silver and gold of the tapestry gleam without the contrasting darker threads? Given this view, when white Europeans focused on nations *outside* Europe, denigration of blacks, orientals, or both was certain to occur, especially during the age of imperialism. As a well-travelled career diplomat in the service of Napoleon III, the older Gobineau became obsessed with the "yellow peril";[24] other Europeans, especially Englishmen but also many Frenchmen, developed a different form of extra-European dualism which emphasized the racial antithesis between the light and the dark-skinned peoples in terms of civilization and barbarism, progress and backwardness, evolution and regression, knowledge and ignorance, morality and immorality, adulthood and childhood. Once Europeans focused on the European nations, which had few orientals or blacks but a significant number of Jews, and the new philosophy joined forces with an old anti-Judaism, the silhouette of the semi-black Semite loomed larger than ever on the public horizon. Before the century came to an end, later Gobinists, mostly in Germany and France (the pattern was different in Britain), inspired by the politics of the day, created a mythical anti-race in the minds of their followers.

According to Jacob Katz, not Gobineau but Ernest Renan (1823–92), the author of the immensely popular *Vie de Jésus,* was the first important Frenchman to recognize the racial superiority of the Aryans over the Semites and to link this concept with traditional anti-Jewish sentiments in French (Catholic) culture.[25] Renan, although an ex-Catholic, was profoundly steeped in Christian religious prejudice, writing, for example, of the Talmud as a work devoid of all morality whose awful squalor forever sets it apart from the sublimity of the Christian New Testament;[26] such an ignoble work was clearly a typical product of the Semitic mind, whereas the New Testament was in all likelihood a product of the Aryan mind. If Jesus was not exactly an Aryan, he was at least a Jew who, paradoxically, was exempt from the faults of his race. Renan held that Jesus's exact racial origins could not be determined (in this respect, Renan was similar to Fichte), but, while it was impossible "to seek to ascertain what blood flowed in the veins of him who has contributed most to efface the distinction of blood in humanity," the *inner* rupture between Jesus and Judaism could not be doubted.[27] Jesus was the spiritual victor over Judaism, arising from a Jewish matrix as Socrates arose from the Sophist schools, as Luther from the Middle Ages, as Lamennais from Catholicism, as Rousseau from the eighteenth century.[28] Whatever the composition of his blood, Renan's Jesus was a non-Semite at least in the important sense that he did not possess an inferior Semitic spirit. A vague rather than explicit racist, the famous French author "moved with remarkable ease past the fine distinctions of race, people, physical type, and linguistic group ... [and] scattered racial terminology somewhat recklessly about his writings, yet he did so in much a manner as to imply the existence of a distinct, identifiable Jewish race."[29]

With his "style ingénieux," Renan lost no opportunity to contrast Aryan and Semitic qualities, contemporary as well as biblical, to the detriment of the latter.[30] For example, following the decisive Prussian victory over the armies of Napoleon III at the battle of Sedan (1870), an event with momentous consequences for French history, he declared that the victory of the Prussians was due to their racial superiority because, unlike the French, they had not stupidly liquidated their (Aryan) aristocracy in the flames of revolution.[31] Other Frenchmen, as we shall see, drew different but equally racist conclusions from the same battle. While the influence of Gobineau and his more tightly formulated version of the Aryan myth on Renan's work is apparent, it is worth mentioning that Renan's fragmentary essay on Jesus and the Talmud appeared several years before the publication of Gobineau's masterwork.[32] Renan was instrumental in the eventual circulation and popularization of Gobineau's ideas in his native country.

Other French writers embroidered Renan's themes and carried them further. Louis Jacolliot, for example, composed an "Aryan Bible" for a universal Aryan religion superior to Christianity in which he ingeniously derived "Jesus" from "Zeus" (Zeus → Iezeus → Isis

→ Jesus).[33] The audacity of this suggestion, as well as its resemblance to the proposals of the extreme German racist ideologues who attempted to invent a new Germanic religion, has gained Jacolliot a minor niche in the racist temple of fame. Only slightly less bizarre was the racial dualism expounded by social radicals such as Gustave Tridon and Albert Regnard to distinguish "Aryan socialism" from "Semitic capitalism."[34] As Communards and disciples of the anarchist August Blanqui, these ultra-leftists created a grotesque fusion of political and biological dogmas. Regnard, who rebuked his follow socialists for neglecting the principles of race, believed that only Aryans were capable of "social renovation" in a decadent age.[35] Later, the distinguished Belgian socialist and senator Edmond Picard, a man who was once described by his admirers as the "intellectual flower" of his nation,[36] decided that Jesus must have been an Aryan because of his antipathy to capitalism, whereas the Jews were the prime bearers of the acquisitive spirit and exploitive instinct in European society.[37] This assertion was borrowed from Karl Marx, Picard's mentor and hero, who, with Ferdinand Lassalle, another great German Socialist of Jewish extraction, was exempted by the Belgian writer from these bad character traits.[38] Marx and Lassalle, in Picard's opinion, were not Jews in a racial sense. They were "no more authentic Jews than Jesus Christ, 'the Aryan *par excellence*' the greatest of the Aryan reformers."[39]

Behind this indictment of capitalism as a Semitic racial trait was the popular nineteenth-century fixation with the Rothschilds, the Jews *par excellence* of the antisemitic imagination. Only socialism could rid Europe of the Semitic-capitalistic plague and restore to European society its lost health and happiness. Jesus, the socialist before socialism, the Marxist before Marxism, the great Aryan Christ, could (with Marx's help, naturally) cure the age of its Semitic affliction by defeating the Rothschilds and their ilk as he had once defeated their ancient Jewish counterparts, the Pharisees and the Sadducees. On this subject, both the reactionary right and the radical left were agreed.

Especially after the fall of the Second Empire, the Aryan myth and its dualistic expressions began to capture a sizable part of public opinion. Indeed, the French nation after 1870 was not unlike the German nation after 1918: a proud people, unexpectedly humiliated in war, had been subjected to an even more humiliating peace which left in its wake a demolished empire, a lost throne, and shattered self-esteem. During the ensuing trauma, as it became apparent that the disaster would be blamed on more than the victorious Prussians, and as vengeful and xenophobic feeling simmered and boiled, racist ideas acquired a sudden new currency in the disturbed atmosphere of the nation, playing havoc with French letters, politics, and science. Stirred by nationalistic sentiments after Sedan, for example, the eminent anthropologist Paul Broca (1824–80) differed from the Germanophile Gobineau and his equally Germanophile disciple Renan by declaring, on scientific grounds, that the "broad-headed" French were racially superior to the "long-headed" Germans because round heads contained larger brains and consequently possessed a better intelligence; Sedan, as a consequence, was entirely misleading, and, in light of the "scientific" evidence (based on extensive cranial measurements and comparisons), certainly no proof of German superiority.[40]

Another nationalistic anthropologist, Broca's colleague Armand de Quatrefages (1810–92), moved by a similar anti-German passion, decided that the Prussians were really Finns and therefore not Aryans at all.[41] Clearly, the French were far superior in racial terms to any quasi-Mongolian people of this type! On the other hand, the reactionary anthropologist Georges Vacher de Lapouge (1854–1936), a disciple of Gobineau who admired the Germans, and, like his master, detested the French Revolution and its egalitarian credo, agreed with Renan that the liquidation of the "eugenic" aristocrats was a racial sin that had weakened France and caused the loss of the war with Prussia.[42] Lapouge's views, however, belong to a somewhat later period, although his anti-egalitarianism was rooted in the racist mood of France in the immediate post-war era.

Nothing illustrates the widespread character of this mood better than the fact that even the egalitarians were captivated by the new ideology. According to Michael Hammond, an entire school of French anthropologists, all "radical republican, anticlerical, evolutionary materialists," incorporated their own progressive political ideals into the evolutionary *telos* itself, while claiming that these goals could be attained only by the more highly developed white race.[43] (As we shall see in the following chapter, this school of thought closely resembled the philosophy of Herbert Spencer.) It is scarcely surprising, then, that many Frenchmen were susceptible to the racial denigration of their Jewish fellow citizens, the so-called Semites. Following the war, Paris was thronged with German-speaking Jewish refugees from the lost provinces of Alsace and Lorraine who had chosen to remain in France. The Third Republic was easily, if circumstantially, associated with Jewish politicians and bankers who were natural scapegoats once its troubles and failures (for example, the Panama Canal scandal of (1892–3) began to accumulate. With the publication of Edouard Drumont's (1844–1917) *La France Juive* in 1886, the new generation of French antisemites received their spiritual testament, making them well-equipped to fight for the soul of the nation. In this "collection of ignoble or obscene stories," as Jean-Paul Sartre later described it, the Jew, especially the Rothschild type of Jew, was protrayed as both the religious and racial enemy of France.[44] Drumont, much more of an extremist than Renan, was far more responsible for promoting racist clichés. Since, unlike Renan who had left the church, he was a Catholic who still attended Mass and apparently took his faith seriously, it is probable that his anti-Jewish feelings were derived in the first instance from traditional Christian teachings, especially the hoary themes of decide, malediction, the degeneracy of Judaism, and the conspiratorial role allegedly played by Jews in the Christian world. Yet Drumont was also modern enough to employ the new language of race when it suited his polemical purposes, intermingling religious and racial stereotypes in a caco-phonous medley. In his eyes, Aryans and Semites were direct op-posites: "The Semite is mercenary, covetous, conspiratorial, crafty, wily; the Aryan is enthusiastic, heroic, chivalrous, unselfish, frank, trusting to the point of naïveté. The Semite is an earthbound creature who scarcely sees anything beyond the present life; the Aryan is a son of heaven ceaselessly preoccupied with higher aspirations; the one lives in reality, the other in an ideal."[45] A paradoxical figure who straddled both the far right and the far left of the political spectrum – he was both a socialist and a "romantic and melancholy conservative"[46] – Drumont combined the various confusions and contradictions of the age. His voice was not the only voice to decry Semitic racial traits in the name of a lofty social ideal, but his socialism, like the National Socialism of Adolf Hitler, was utterly subservient to his nationalism and, in the final analysis, little more than a farce. The comparison with Hitler is wholly appropriate for Drumont was a fascist before the rise of fascism, and only the Nazi Führer ever exceeded the notorious journalist of the Dreyfus era in the pitch and fervour of his racial Manichaeism. In Hitler's case, antisemitism was elevated to the status of a cosmological principle.[47]

INFECTED CATHOLICISM

Alienation was the womb of Gobineau's philosophy and the reason for its appeal to alienated groups in French society. The second estate, the nobility – or what was left of it – could not forgive the bourgeoisie for the 1789 revolution and consequently was filled with a festering resentment of republican France and its political egali-tarianism. The first estate, the Roman Catholic church, never succeeded in regaining its pre-1789 status, in spite of the Concordat with Napoleon (1801) and disingenuous declarations during the reigns of Louis XVIII and Charles X, and consequently was filled with a similar dislike. While some Catholics managed to accommodate themselves to the political order established by the revolution as early as the civil constitution (1790–3), and other Catholics accommodated themselves to the Second Republic well before the age of *Ralliement* (the acceptance of republican France urged in 1892 by Pope Leo XIII), throughout the nineteenth century most of the church remained emotionally wedded to the old regime. As a religious institution obsessed by memories of its former glory, it was highly susceptible to negative opinions of the present and apt – given the character of Christian theology – to read a diabolical significance into the events deemed responsible for its misfortunes. This negative mood was not alleviated by the anti-clerical legislation of the Third Republic (1879–83), whose government as a consequence was perceived as godless and Jew-ridden by the angry Catholics. Already anti-Jewish on religious and theological grounds. Catholics who by now represented a counter-culturel in France, became more and more receptive to ideas that connected the most ancient enemies of the true faith with what it regarded as the most evil episode in French history: the 1789 revolution. The church had always known that the Jews were devil-instigated; after 1800 it knew that the revolution was devil-instigated; and after 1870 it rapidly formed the opinion that the government of the Third Republic was devil-instigated. It seemed quite plausible, therefore, to read modern French history as an elaborate Jewish conspiracy with the devil pulling the strings. This is exactly what Drumont did.

Except for a single early writing (possibly fabricated by the Napoleonic police), however, the anti-revolutionary ideologues did not initially ascribe the revolution to Jewish machinations.[48] Instead, the French Masons were blamed, together with the short-lived Bavarian *Illuminati*. The first generation of suspicious and resentful churchmen saw freemasonry, a secret brotherhood with rationalistic, mystical, and suspected republican propensities, as a natural devil's agent.[49] (The Jews, in fact, played no active part in French public life during the revolutionary epoch.) During the troubled year of 1848, the Masonic lodges of both France and Germany were denounced as "subverters of the stability of state, society and church."[50] Because some Masons were also Jews, and because the Jews had long been regarded in Catholic lore as conspirators against Christendom, the creation of a Jewish-Masonic conspiracy was a logical next step. Henri Gougenot des Mousseaux, a Catholic polemicist, took this step in 1869, on the eve of Sedan, linking the Jews to the Masons as the co-authors of France's woes.[51] Protestants, incidentally, were also included in the indictment, but they never acquired the same mythical significance for the Catholic polemicists. A more ancient antagonism excluded them from the pride of place reserved for those whom Ernest Jouin, a twentieth-century cleric and the author of a later anti-Jewish anti-Masonic text, identified in Augustinian terms as the "city of evil" and therefore the true enemies of the "city of God," the Roman Catholic church.[52]

As Catholic resentment of the secular state mounted during the Third Republic, with the nation suffering from the psychic and political wounds inflicted by the Franco-Prussian war, old anti-Jewish motifs were replayed with dangerous variations. Fadiey Lovsky employs the phrase "antisemitism of resentment" to describe the manner in which the church's nostalgia for "Christian" France and all of its imaginary attributes, sharpened by the anguish of state persecution, became the portal through which newly-contrived racial doctrines entered the citadel of French Catholicism.[53] Even prior to Gobineau, a certain racial flavour had already started to creep into the pages of Catholic social criticism.[54] Now it ran rampant. Catholics, especially provincial curés, were easily terrorized by nightmares of a Jewish-Masonic-Protestant plot against Catholic (i.e., true) France, an alliance in which the Jews, of course, were the real *bête noire*. Three conspiracies were fused into a single conspiracy with a single archdemon – international Jewry – in league with the great Father of all lies, Satan himself. This curious trinitarianism, moreover, was encouraged by the existence of the *Alliance israélite universelle*, a Jewish philanthropic organization founded in 1860 which most Catholics saw as still another secret society with essentially anti-Catholic intentions. Then, to make matters worse, in 1884 Pope Leo XIII breathed Augustinian dualism into his denunciation of Freemasonry:

When through the envy of the devil the human race had miserably fallen away from God, the Creator, the Dispenser of all heavenly gifts, it divided itself into two separate and hostile camps, of which the one wars perpetually for truth and virtue, and the other for everything that is antagonistic to truth and virtue. The one is the kingdom of God upon earth, – that is, the true Church of Jesus Christ ... the other is the kingdom of Satan ... All through the ages these cities have fought, one with the other, with many weapons, and in many forms of strife, though not always with the same fierceness or the same energy. In our own time, the enemies of God, aided and strengthened by the widely-spread and firmly-knit society of the Masons, seem to have united to make a supreme effort.[55]

If even the great social pope of the nineteenth century felt this degree of anti-Masonic antipathy, it is not surprising that his French co-religionists, for whom Masons and Jews had become virtually equivalent, were highly predisposed to regard the latter as both the religious enemies of Christendom and the racial enemies of France – a more or less equivalent charge. Racist terminology, now in wide circulation, could be readily exploited by Catholics such as Drumont to stress the qualitative difference between Christian Aryans and non-Christian Semites and the political implications of their mutual opposition. As far as the church was concerned, racial language was initially only an intriguing new weapon against the hated republic. The weapon soon, however, became an end as well as a means, and Catholics who borrowed Gobinist ideas in order to embellish a deeply ingrained religious and social prejudice found it an easy transition from theological anti-Judaism to racist antisemitism. Eventually, the latter virtually replaced the former as a popular mode of speech, although the religious dimension in French racism was never wholly eliminated. When, for example, Léon Blum became prime minister of France in 1936, there was more indignation in some quarters at the spectacle of a Semite presiding over a Gallic-Roman nation than at a Jew presiding over a Christian nation.[56]

Drumont's appeal was primarily to middle-class Catholics and the lower clergy. The number of imitators he inspired in these circles only demonstrates further the drift from religious to racial ideas in Catholic France. From 1894 to 1906 during the famous Dreyfus affair (the arrest and trial of Alfred Dreyfus, a Jewish officer, on a charge of treason), when the accumulated tensions of French society finally resulted in open conflict, the already anti-Jewish Catholic press visibly escalated the racial element in its polemic against the Dreyfusards. The Assumptionist journal *La Croix*, for example, substituted the "French race" for the "Christian race" as the true enemy of the Jews,[57] and clerics such as Henri Desportes and Henri Delassus chose racial rather than religious images to express their animosity.[58] In true racist fashion, a later ecclesiastic, after identifying the eternal contest between God and Satan with the temporal contest between Catholics and Jews, rejected conversion as an answer to the Jewish problem because converted Jews could not be redeemed from their bad (racial) traits.[59] The ghosts of the Spanish Old Christians have whispered in his ear!

By 1942, Henri de Lubac was obliged to defend the integrity of the holy scriptures against a racist "Marcionism" in the French church that was apparently determined to place an "Aryan" New Testament opposite a "Semitic" Old Testament.[60] During this sinister period in European history, the racist ingredient in French Catholicism and French right-wing politics became particularly menacing. Not only did the collaborators of the Vichy regime comply with the antisemitic policies of the Nazi invaders, but they actually engaged in persecutions of their own with less opposition from the Christian community in France than might have been expected.[61] As in Germany, the church was too contaminated by nationalism, racism, and antisemitism to act effectively against a murderous state.

The full extent of this contamination, and the ideological purpose that it served, has been thoroughly analyzed by Stephen Wilson in his study of the definitive years of the Third Republic.[62] In order to hold the perils of modernity at bay, alienated Frenchmen incorporated nationalistic, racist, and antisemitic slogans into an anti-modern worldview in which the "Christian" values of the past – a highly idealized past that never existed except in their own imaginations – were contrasted with the anti-Christian values of the present in the most radical fashion possible. They saw themselves as custodians of the nation's moral and spiritual treasures and invested "Christian" France, the France that once had been and was no more, except within their hearts, with all of the virtues that were deemed to have disappeared from the contemporary republic. Rural society (idealized) was exalted over urban society, i.e., the pure Christian countryside over the corrupt Jewish city; pre-capitalist industry (once again idealized) was exalted over industrial capitalism; i.e., the peasant and artisan over the factory worker; order, hierarchy, and absolutism were exalted over disorder, egalitarianism, and relativism, i.e., a system with firm moral boundaries over a system in which change and revolution were endemic. In particular, the neo-Catholics feared the emancipation of women, sexual liberation, and the dissolution of the patriarchal family. Significantly, they turned to national symbols such as the army, with they associated with order, hierarchy, and male beauty: all racist concepts. Thoroughly dissatisfied with the modern age and its rationalistic ethos, they turned for comfort to tales of an older time – the saga of the nation itself – as a refuge from the dangerous new horizons that loomed in their path. We are dealing, in other words, with the emotional and ideological roots of French fascism and all of its assorted evils.

JESUS AND JUPITER

Those French Catholics who turned to Gobineau's doctrines in the hope of purifying France of its internal enemies soon had reason to doubt the wisdom of their choice. Having admitted the serpent to their inner sanctum, they found themselves wrapped in its coils. Racist theories are not easily domesticated; they can be directed against Christians as well as Jews and, as we saw in chapter two, even against Christianity itself. In France, this danger was made evident by Charles Maurras (1868–1952), one of the founders of the royalist political movement *Action Française* and an apostle of counter-revolution throughout his long and turbulent career. A disciple of Gobineau and, like Gobineau, a nominal Catholic who approved of Catholicism for cultural rather than religious reasons, i.e., as a fundamental part of the French or "Latin" identity, Maurras supported the church until in 1926 Pius XI finally forced him to choose between his political allegiance and his ecclesiastical allegiance.[63] Not surprisingly, Maurras selected the party over the church and became bitterly anti-clerical. Even before his rupture with the papacy, however, his use of Christian symbols was highly unorthodox, and, as we shall see, profoundly corrupted by racist ideology. Perhaps the choice between Christianity and racism was not difficult for a man whose religious convictions were scarcely *une force majeure* to begin with, but, for Catholic racists who did not wish to dispense with either Catholicism or royalism, the pope's condemnation of Maurras and the *Action Française* provoked a crisis of faith. Should the pope be obeyed or disobeyed? Although Pius XI was neither a racist nor an antisemite, his attack on Maurras and his movement was probably motivated more by his desire to reassert his authority over his French domain and his dislike of Maurras' agnosticism than by a dislike of political reaction as such.[64]

Like his German Christian counterparts of a slightly later era, Maurras made the nation and its sacred history – the history of anti-revolutionary, Catholic, and aristocratic France – the matrix of his theology. Like Hirsch in Germany, he wanted to found the church on this rock, and on this rock alone. For him, the *Roman* rather than the Christian character of Roman Catholicism was paramount since the classical tradition was an essential element in the French national genius. Thus France and Italy, the Latin-Catholic nations, were endowed with special significance as the repositories of true (i.e., classical) civilization and the defenders of its heritage.[65] Maurras was bitterly anti-German as a consequence of the Franco-Prussian war and the loss of Alsace and Lorraine that followed. Hating the Germans as much as he hated the Jews, he revised the Aryan myth along French nationalistic lines in the same spirit if not in the same manner as the anthropologists Broca and Quatrefages; no German sympathies were acceptable to a Frenchman filled with revulsion toward the new imperial (and Protestant) Germany inaugurated by Bismarck in, of all places, the great palace of the French kings at Versailles.

Not the Teutonic but the "Latin" race was the proper object of national glorification.

It was Maurras' mission to make the French realize this and to direct the gaze of his compatriots toward the Latinized descendants of the Gauls and the Romans, augmented by those assimilated barbarian elements whose spiritual genius was still apparent in modern French culture. From this "Gallo-Roman type." he argued (in curious agreement with Sieyès), one proceeds "in order to conceive and define the French type."[66] Once defined, the latter supplied or should have supplied the French with the correct mirror in which to enjoy the reflection of their own faces. Not surprisingly, Maurras was contemptuous of the biblical, Hebraic, or Jewish aspects of Christianity, regarding the early (Jewish) church as a "semitic leprosy" in the great body of Graeco-Roman civilization.[67] Jesus, on the other hand, at least the "Christ of the [Roman] Catholic tradition," was quite another matter; he was nothing less than a Latin god – the "sovereign Jupiter who was crucified for us on earth."[68] His atoning death, Maurras seems to have believed, was accomplished on behalf of the French race alone!

Another godparent of French fascism, Maurice Barrès (1862–1923) adapted Fichte's ideas in the formulation of his own concept of "integral nationalism."[69] He also advocated a reconciliation between the old pagan deities and the Catholic saints which would unite Catholic religious feeling with "the spirit of the earth."[70] Only Semitism, Barrès believed, was monotheistic; Christianity was really polytheistic, worshipping the Son, the Virgin, and the local saints.[71] It was thus a more authentic religion for the French, at least in its Roman form. Like Protestantism in Germany, Catholicism in France was easily reconstructed along racist lines once the need for a sense of rootedness and a myth of national origin became acute among the intelligentsia. Of necessity, this involved a radical alteration in the main components of ecclesiastical doctrine, beginning with christology. In the end, not even the semblance of biblical faith remained to those who followed this path.

CHAPTER FOUR

The Anglo-Saxon Christ

Tacitus was also the progenitor of Anglo-Saxon racism, at least as far as its core assumptions are concerned. The Germanic myth was drawn into the social and political conflicts of the English civil war era by seventeenth-century writers who, somewhat fancifully, interpreted the war in racial as well as in class terms.[1] According to these sectarians, England (like France) consisted of two nations, Normans and Saxons, and the contest between king and parliament pitted these two races against each other in mortal combat. Charles I was seen as no less a "Norman" intruder than his eleventh-century ancestor William I, and his parliamentary opponents portrayed themselves as the true English or "Saxon" race – the descendants of the Conqueror's enemies at the Battle of Hastings. England was equated with Israel as an enslaved nation ruled by "kings, lords, judges, justices, bailiffs and ... violent people" whom the "Norman bastard William" and his "colonels, captains, inferior officers and common soldiers" had inflicted on the poor "English Israelites" in order to imprison, rob, and murder them.[2]

Not surprisingly, in light of this analysis, political liberty, that most precious of all precious objects, was identified with the Germanic or Saxon origins of the English nation, notably with the Saxon chieftains Hengist and Horsa who supposedly carried the sacred torch of freedom from Germany to England after the withdrawal of the Roman legions. With the ascension to the throne of William and Mary in the Glorious Revolution of 1688, the struggles of the seventeenth century subsided following the establishment of constitutional monarchy. The supporters of the new regime saw its political principles as the embodiment of Germanic liberty inherited from the forests of old Germany.[3] In the eighteenth century, David Hume was a firm advocate of this view;[4] in the nineteenth century, men such as Charles Kingsley, instilled with romantic feelings, were infatuated with the myth.[5] Even Benjamin Disraeli, who was certainly not Anglo-Saxon, fell in with the mood of the epoch by endorsing the genius of a system that elevated the "Rights of Englishmen" above the "Rights of Men,"[6] declaring, before Count Gobineau, that "all is race: there is no other truth!"[7] The British Gobineau, however, was a disgruntled Scottish anatomist and medical instructor named Robert Knox (1798–1862) who provided Disraeli's dictum with a scientific, or pseudo-scientific, rationale. Published shortly before Gobineau's *Essai*, Knox's lectures on *The Races of Men* (1850) came independently to the same broad conclusion. The Saxon race myth, hitherto a social and political fantasy, became a truth of nature.

THE BRITISH GOBINEAU

Despite his scientific orientation, Knox, like his French counterpart, was motivated by personal passions of a decidedly non-scientific character. Another alienated individual (he was embittered by a scandal in his medical career)[8] who intensely disliked his age and its rulers, Knox glorified the Saxon – his own chosen racial alter ego – as "nature's democrat" in undemocratic Britain in much the same fashion, although with diametrically opposed results, as Gobineau glorified the Frankish (Aryan) aristocracy.[9] Gobineau, however, identified Teutonic liberty with feudal privilege, whereas Knox identified it with political democracy; consequently, for Gobineau the rise of egalitarianism was a sign of racial decay, while for Knox it was a sign of racial progress. Gobineau was forced to seek solace for the ills of the present in the past, but Knox was able to turn to the future, giving his prognosis an optimistic cast entirely lacking in his more illustrious French contemporary.

Knox, however, was no less a racist; indeed, in some respects, especially in his dislike of Jews, he was more virulent than Gobineau.[10] Saxons, and Saxons alone, according to Knox, possess an innate (racial) capacity for true democracy. An ardent republican in Victorian England, he regarded the British monarchy, even in the nineteenth century, as a Norman imposition on a Saxon people, apparently borrowing from the language of the seventeenth-century sectarians. The monarchy, he declared, was fit only for "dynasty-loving" Celts and entirely "antagonistic to the Saxon race it governs."[11] The current state of affairs was clearly contrary to nature and could not endure indefinitely. Indeed, in Knox's eyes, the modern Saxons, those perfect duplicates of their great ancestors "who started from the woods of Germany to meet Caesar on the Rhine," were already smashing the shackles of tyranny by demanding free institutions in Britain, in southern Africa, and in Upper Canada (presumably he had the Mackenzie rebellion of 1837 in mind).[12] The "Norman" dynasty, with its "sham constitution," had been driven from the rest of the North American continent during the American Revolution, suggesting that greater things were to follow. Some day, the Saxons would triumph over all of their rivals; some day, Knox predicted – in this case with a certain amount of prescience – a mighty republican empire would establish itself on the soil of America and therefrom rule the earth![13]

In this fashion, Knox indulged in a racial dream of an earthly apotheosis of the Saxon race as the bearers of all true progress in history and, with the Slavs (whom he also admired for their intellectual abilities), the highest and noblest specimens of humanity. Their future was virtually predestined. By Saxons, Knox, who, in spite of his lowland Scottish background, did not regard himself as a Celt, was referring to the British middle class of which he was a part. The Normans and the Celts were respectively the upper and lower classes of British society which either would not or could not recognize his important talents. Like Gobineau, his true subject was himself.

His theory was presented as science. In contrast to his American contemporary Samuel Morton, Knox was not a paleontologist, and hence proposed a somewhat different explanation for the inequality of the human races. Dismissing the question of the origin of life as beyond the powers of human inquiry, he turned instead to the question of its variety, especially the variety of human types as reflected in the races as well as among individuals. A pre-evolutionary thinker, he regarded nature as a great primordial unity or universal scheme of things governed by essential laws of "formation" and "deformation."[14] This led him to the concept of "transcendental anatomy," or the notion that the past, present, and future of the entire organic realm is recapitulated in the life of the embryo; the individual creature, in other words, passes through a succession of forms that foreshadow every stage in what would later be called the evolutionary process (although, as a pre-Darwinian scientist, Knox thought of the human form in Platonic terms as immutable and final rather than as changing and unfinished).[15] Fish, birds, reptiles, mammals – all are linked with humans, and their characteristics are seen in one stage or another of the developing human fetus, which "by structure and by plan," is intimately connected to everything that "has lived or yet may live."[16] When the embryo perfectly recapitulates the entire process, the result is perfect, but when, as a consequence of circumstances that Knox did not claim to be able to understand, the process is arrested at some stage – for example, the reptilian stage – deformation results. Webbed fingers, cleft palates, etc., among individuals reflect primitive levels of development in nature that correspond to those of certain reptiles, birds, or other creatures. These deformations, moreover, account for racial differences between the different branches of the human species, even if no one can say when or by what means the various races were initially divided from each other.

For Knox, different cultures with different languages and religions, as well as different physical and mental characteristics, were rooted in transcendental anatomy. These racial communities are far from equal: some are less deformed than others, and the less deformed innately despise the more deformed. Saxons and Slavs, according to his studies, are the least deformed (although neither race is perfect), and, among these highly endowed white races, the finest examples of the female form supplied Knox with his vision of the "perfection of Nature's works; the absolutely perfect; the beautiful, the highest manifestation of abstract life, clothed in a physical form, adapted to the corresponding minds of her race and species."[17]

The British Gobineau, whose book, incidentally, was admired by Charles Darwin,[18] contributed in no small measure to the future course of Anglo-Saxon racism by supplying the next generation of British and American race supremacists with scientific ammunition for their political claims. To use Loren R. Graham's terminology, he was a striking example of a scientist with an "expansionist" rather than a "restrictionist" view of science: a scientist who, instead of remaining within the tight and narrow boundaries of science, allows his scientific conclusions to overrun the whole of human knowledge without acknowledging any boundaries.[19]

For Knox, as for Disraeli, everything could be reduced to the question of race and race alone. With this conviction firmly in mind, he had no difficulty explaining the anatomy of history and society as well as the anatomy of the human body. After Knox, there were few restrictionists in the scientific and social thought of the nineteenth century. Evolutionary theory made the expansionist temptation virtually irresistible, although, oddly enough, the great proponent of evolution, Charles Darwin, was at least to some extent an exception to this statement.

EVOLUTION AND RACE

Darwin's *Origin of Species* was published in 1859. The term "natural selection" was soon in common use and neither science, philosophy, nor religion was the same again. Darwin, it is generally agreed, was not a racist, although occasional references to Aryans and Semites are found in his writings, and in his later publication *The Descent of Man* he argued for as much "open competition" as possible among human beings in order to promote natural selection and thereby enhance the future of the species.[20] In spite, however, of his fascination with human diversity – a fascination that may have been stirred by a certain amount of racial feeling – he stressed human unity, which he saw as stemming from a remote common progenitor. Linked by shared ancestors, even the races that differed most from each other in physical attributes seemed to possess similar intellectual capabilities which indicated their common descent.[21]

The danger, therefore, was not from Darwin but from his admirers, who began to draw extravagant conclusions from the evolutionary hypothesis and its attendant concepts of natural selection and the struggle for existence. It was suddenly all too easy to improve on Knoxian doctrines by embroidering the rapidly growing Saxon myth with these Darwinian themes, finding proof of Anglo-Saxon racial superiority in the triumphs of the British during the age of empire and of the Americans during the age of continental expansion. If natural selection marked the path of human evolution, it was obvious which race was gaining the most ground in the cosmic struggle, and which race, therefore, most deserved to succeed. Surely the success of the Anglo-Saxons, two nations but a single people, demonstrated their racial superiority, and surely their racial superiority justified the growing titanism of the two great Anglo-Saxon nations. The Social Darwinians could have it both ways.

The term "Saxondom," later amended to Anglo-Saxondom, was coined by another British republican, Charles Wentworth Dilke (1843–1911), whose paean *Greater Britain*, on the impending global dominance of the Saxons over the "cheaper peoples" of the earth, suffused the Anglo-American future with a roseate glow.[22] By 1970, he asserted, Saxondom, i.e., all the English-speaking nations but especially Britain and the United States, will have reduced its non-Saxon rivals to the status of pigmies. "Chili [sic], La Plata, and Peru must eventually become English; the Red Indian race that now occupies those countries cannot stand against our colonists; and the future of the table-lands of Africa and that of Japan and of China is as clear."[23] The superior people, moving from one remarkable feat to another, will steadily plant the principles of Saxon liberty, "so dear to the freedom of mankind," and Saxon political institutions among the "dark-skinned" races.[24]

Not mother England, however, but the United States of America with its republican constitution was the heart and most lofty expression of this liberty, since, according to Dilke (as to Knox) republicanism is the essence of true democracy. The ancient Saxons presumably were republicans, electing their kings and making them accountable to their tribal assemblies. Britain should emulate the American example and shed its obsolete and decidedly non-Saxon monarchy. Modern Saxondom, in Dilke's futuristic vision, was to be a vast new tribal confederacy of Saxon republics – a "greater Britain" – whose progress nothing could impede. The latter-day Saxons would surely inherit and civilize the earth, exactly as their racial ancestors had once inherited and civilized the Europe of the Dark Ages after the fall of the Roman empire.

In the latter half of the nineteenth century it was easy for Englishmen and Americans to entertain such grandiose expectations, although they did not always share the same constitutional premises. Dilke's assumptions, however, were sometimes carried to ridiculous lengths, especially in American hands. Thus, during the revival of Anglo-Saxon literary and linguistic studies in American universities in the same general period, a Yale professor declared that republican Americans were better students in this field than royalist Englishmen (obviously, he did not have Dilke in mind) because the United States was a more authentic Saxon democracy than monarchical England.[25] Perhaps he was only echoing Fichte, for whom language, race, and culture formed a single compound. Certainly, as early as Thomas Jefferson, there was a tendency in American thought to identify the roots of American democracy with pre-Norman England and therefore with the Saxon origins of the English language itself.[26]

Another British republican, admirer of America's constitution, exponent of the Anglo-Saxon myth, and evolutionary theorist, was the influential philosopher Herbert Spencer (1820–1903). It was Spencer, not Darwin, who coined the term "survival of the fittest" which was so crucial to Social Darwinism and so fraught with un-anticipated and dangerous meanings, although Spencer did not intend his refinement of natural selection as a crude vindication of the mastery of the strong.[27] On the contrary, his instincts were highly pacific and informed by Enlightenment faith in the infinite possibilities of human and social betterment through the great march of cosmic time. Naively, he believed that human nature (by which he generally meant Anglo-Saxon nature) was shifting from egoism to altruism as the Industrial Age unfolded since industrialization produces social equilibrium as a consequence of the need for close internal co-operation between the different segments of society, and social equilibrium creates the conditions for international peace and harmony.[28] Peace, therefore, marks the path of progress, and progress charts the course of evolution, which is not, as natural selection might make it seem, a haphazard affair but a case of linear progression.

Unfortunately, Spencer mingled this bright and happy optimism with a certain amount of racial language. During an lecture tour of the United States in 1882, he told the Americans that the "eventual mixture of the allied varieties of the Aryan race forming the [US] population" would "produce a finer type of man than has hitherto existed ... more plastic, more adaptable, more capable of undergoing the modifications needful for complete social life."[29] This curious prediction evidently rested on the equally curious assumption that, since the Americans had allegedly created the highest form of the highest kind of political institution, i.e., republican democracy, they must represent the highest form of the highest kind of man on the evolutionary scale, i.e., Anglo-Saxon (Aryan) man. It also rested on Lamarckian assumptions about the inheritability of acquired characteristics that not all evolutionary thinkers, including Darwin, endorsed. Not surprisingly, Spencer's lectures and philosophical writings became immensely popular in the United States where his visit was a spectacular success. Despite the racist elements in his thought, he was largely innocent of overt racism and only sketched these ideas in a vague, and according to J. D. Y. Peel, somewhat confused manner.[30] However, the notion that life is a process of adaptation in which only the more adaptable or fit species survive, leaving the unfit to fall away and perish, had social, political, and racial implications that the less idealistic Social Darwinians did not fail to notice. Even Spencer believed that the poor should be eliminated as nature's outcasts.[31]

If the Anglo-Saxons were producing superior political institutions, and if a higher type of human was evolving in their midst, it was reasonable to suppose that they had emerged early as front-runners in the cosmic contest. To the American Spencerians, this headstart was easily explained: their ancestral brains had developed larger craniums and therefore a larger mental capacity during the struggles of pre-history, allowing, as Spencer would have said, further differentiation and specialization. In fact, only Anglo-Saxons (Aryans, Caucasions, etc.) were really still evolving; the lower races had either completed their evolutionary course already, or were hopelessly behind in the contest.[32] As atavistic misfits in the modern industrialized world, they were seen by the Spencerians as "mentally incapable of shouldering the burdens of a complex civilization," and would probably sink into extinction in the not too distant future.[33]

This thesis, a compound of Mortonian craniology, Knoxian transcendental anatomy, Darwinian biology, rationalistic faith, and simple
unadulterated Anglo-American chauvinism, naturally appealed to
the age. Spencer's American disciple John Fiske (1842–1901), while
he regarded the term "Anglo-Saxon" as slovenly and spoke instead
of the "English" race, composed one of the most lyrical tributes to
Anglo-Saxon manifest destiny ever penned.[34] From its remote origins
in the Teutonic village, the Aryan instinct for democracy gave birth
to English self-government – "the secret of that boundless vitality
which has given to men of English speech the uttermost parts of
the earth for an inheritance" – and subsequently to the New England
town meeting as its latter-day manifestation.[35] With the advent of
the American republic, "an astonished world" could behold the
wonder of "two Englands" in place of one, "prepared to work with
might and main toward the political regeneration of mankind."[36]
Soon the Anglo-Saxon colossus would spread his mighty limbs over
the entire surface of the globe, covering the hemispheres "from the
rising to the setting sun" until every nation "not already the seat of
an old civilization shall become English in its language, in its political
habits and traditions, and to a predominant extent in the blood of
its people."[37] The African continent, for example, will finally be
occupied by the English race, which will fill it with "populous cities
and flourishing farms, with railroads and telegraphs";[38] the native
peoples, no doubt, without any interference on the part of the most
highly evolved race, will suffer an appropriate Spencerian fate.

In this fashion, the great antithesis between civilization and barbarism, progress and backwardness, evolution and regression,
knowledge and ignorance, morality and immorality, adulthood and
childhood, etc., all elaborated in terms of racial dualism, found repeated expression as the cardinal tenet of the Anglo-Saxon credo.
Was not the advance of Anglo-Saxondom much the same thing as
the advance of nature and humanity as a whole? Who, then could
reasonably oppose British imperialism and American expansionism
– in Richard Hofstadter's phrase, the coming "Pax Anglo-Americana"
– since human betterment itself was at stake?[39] Furthermore, the
darker-skinned peoples, in theory if not always in fact, were seldom
regarded by the Anglo-Saxons as racial enemies, to be liquidated by
the sword. Rather, they were children, and, in the eyes of Christian
England and Christian America, the objects of benevolence and pa-
ternal care. Of course, as Thomas Carlyle's thoughts on the West
Indian "niggers" with their "beautiful muzzles up to the ears in
pumpkins" illustrate, Anglo-Saxon sentiments were not always
benevolent.[40]

CHRISTIANITY AND THE ANGLO-SAXON DREAM

The religious fervour of Josiah Strong (1847–1916), one of the fathers of the American social gospel and a Protestant with characteristic liberal convictions, was thoroughly infected by the "burgeoning pride in Anglo-Saxonism" that swept post-bellum America.[41] Liberal Christianity, by definition, implied an intellectual receptivity to scientific and philosophical ideas, and this implied receptivity to the racial elements that were embedded in evolutionary thought as interpreted by Spencer and his disciples. "To have denied the superiority of the Anglo-Saxon would have been to have flown in the face of scientific fact and to have identified oneself with the Biblical literalists who were the bane of the Social Gospel movement."[42]

Consequently Strong, and to a lesser extent the other theologians and preachers of social reform in America, or what Walter Rauschenbusch later called "Christianizing" the social order,[43] chose science – the scripture of nature, wherein the holy spirit is also immanent – over the wooden textual literalism of their conservative foes. Race, as we have seen, had become an attested fact of nature, and the Anglo-Saxons had become the most highly evolved race; it only remained, therefore, to relate this scientifically revealed knowledge to the great theme of divine providence, and to seek God's purpose in so guiding the hand of the evolutionary process. Here, Strong was certain. Was it a historic coincidence that the "great reformation of the sixteenth century originated among a Teutonic, rather than a Latin people?" No, only the "fire of liberty burning in the Saxon heart" could have flamed up against papal oppression.[44] Was it a historic coincidence that modern America rather than the "pretty island" of England was rapidly seizing the "scepter of controlling influence" in the ever-expanding Anglo-Saxon world?[45] No, for the American type of Anglo-Saxon man possessed the "finer nervous organization," and everyone knew that the "finest nervous organization" produced the "highest civilization."[46] America, as a result, was not merely the chosen nation, and the American (not the English) race the chosen race as far as Strong was concerned, but, according to him, God, "with infinite wisdom and skill," was carefully training the American Anglo-Saxons "for an hour sure to come in the world's future."[47]

Indeed, for a long time God had carefully prepared the path for the coming of the divine kingdom by directing the racial evolution of his creatures until the Anglo-Saxon race was fashioned, uniting within itself the best characteristics of the preceding races: Greek individualism, Roman organization, and Hebrew spirituality.[48] Such a remarkable fruition was clearly intended for some inspired purpose; in carrying their civilization "like a ring of Saturn – a girdle of light – around the globe,"[49] the Anglo-Saxons were surely fulfilling the divine will by inaugurating a radical new stage in world history: "a single supreme civilization ... the perfection of which will be the Kingdom fully come."[50] It was all transparent to the eyes of faith, or at least to Josiah Strong. It was so transparent that, in spite of his profound social conscience, Strong demonstrated no greater concern for those races which did *not* have the good fortune to belong to the Anglo-Saxon family than any other Social Darwinian.

Long before the thousand millions are here, the mighty *centrifugal* tendency, inherent in this stock and strengthened in the United States, will assert itself. Then this race of unequaled energy, with all the majesty of numbers and the might of wealth behind it – the representative, let us hope, of the largest liberty, the purest Christianity, the highest civilization — having developed peculiarly aggressive traits calculated to impress its institutions upon mankind, will spread itself over the earth. If I read not amiss, this powerful race will move down upon Mexico, down upon Central and South America, out upon the islands of the sea, over upon Africa and beyond. And can any one doubt that the result of this competition of races will be the "survival of the fittest"? ... Nothing can save the inferior race but a ready and pliant assimilation. Whether the feebler and more abject races are going to be regenerated and raised up, is already very much of a question. What if it should be God's plan to people the world with better and finer material? ... To this result no war of extermination is needful; the contest is not one of arms but of vitality and civilization ... Whether the extinction of inferior races before the advancing Anglo-Saxon seems to the reader sad or otherwise, it certainly appears probable ... Thus, while on this continent God is training the Anglo-Saxon race for its mission, a complemental work has been in progress in the great world beyond. God has two hands. Not only is he preparing in our civilization the die with which to stamp the nations, but, by what Southey called the "timing of Providence", he is preparing mankind to receive our impress.[51]

Jesus, of course, was not an Anglo-Saxon, at least not in so many words, although the affinity between the most perfect and most spiritual individual who ever lived and the pure *spiritual* Christianity of the highest and most advanced race was certainly no coincidence.[52] The Anglo-Saxons, for Strong, having inherited the Hebrew gift of spirituality, were in this sense the true modern Hebrews, not the post-biblical Jews. Indeed, like many Christian theologians, the

American writer drew a radical distinction between the biblical Hebrews and the post-biblical Jews, regarding the former as proto-Christians and the latter as anti-Christians, the bigoted adherents of a ritualistic and empty religion.[53] Like Lagarde, he described Jesus as their antithesis, finding an "absolute contrariety between his teachings and rabbinism."[54] As the "generic" man, the central figure of Christianity so transcended his own age and all ages that the Jewish imagination could never have conceived of or understood such sublime perfection.[55] (Strong, however, no doubt as a consequence of his Anglo-Saxon lineage, rose to the occasion with admirable ease, judging from the lengthy panegryric in his book *The New Era*).[56] In the end, since "to be a Christian and an Anglo-Saxon and an American" was for this theologian "to stand on the very mountain-top of privilege,"[57] it is difficult to avoid the conclusion that his "authoritative teacher" (Christ)[58] was really an American as well, or at least a proto-American in addition to being a proto-Christian and proto-Anglo-Saxon. Why not? After all, Spencer had predicted that the Americans would produce the finest specimen of the human species, and the most perfect man that ever lived should certainly be placed at the pinnacle of the evolutionary scale.

While Strong expressed his Anglo-Saxon prometheanism in far more forceful and extreme language than the other Protestant liberals of the day, men such as Horace Bushnell, Washington Gladden, and Walter Rauschenbusch were also tainted by the same ideology.[59] Rauschenbusch, for example, was explicit about his belief in the Aryan myth[60] and occasionally spoke of both Aryan and Anglo-Saxon superiority in the political and religious arenas, arguing that such institutions as communal rather than private property were distinctive "marks of the Aryan race" with its "virility" and talent for freedom,[61] and that there was a peculiar affinity between Anglo-Saxondom and the Christian faith. "In the Anglo-Saxon communities especially the spirit of religion has blended with the spirit of freedom; or rather, here the spirit of Christianity has been set free sufficiently to do its work in the field of political life, and has found one great outlook for its power in creating a passionate love for freedom and equality."[62] Rauschenbusch naturally preferred "Anglo-Saxon caution" (in social reform) to the "French balloon of abstract principles and logical schemes,"[63] and, apparently for this reason, rejected continental socialism.

In expressing these convictions, the fathers of the American social gospel were tapping the deepest wells of the American collective memory, the sources of the sacred myth of the nation itself. American puritanism, with its sense of special election in which the latter-day

Israelites (the Mayflower generation) crossed a latter-day desert (the Atlantic Ocean) in flight from a latter-day Egypt (Europe) in quest of a latter-day promised land (the virgin continent), for possession of which they battled latter-day Canaanites (the Indian tribes), almost certainly informed the thought of nineteenth-century Anglo-Saxon theologians even when, like Rauschenbusch, they could hardly claim to be direct descendants of the founding generation. But that, of course, did not matter.

During the same era, Protestants in the American south, influenced directly by Strong, employed the same myth to intensify public resistance to the notion of racial equality for blacks and promote their *de facto* re-enslavement by grafting the more scientific rationale for white supremacy onto the ante-bellum biblical myth of Ham.[64] Thus, as H. Shelton Smith has pointed out, a new racial orthodoxy followed the abolition of slavery with the specific purpose of destroying the fruits of emancipation;[65] a pattern, incidentally, remarkably similar to the rise of another racial orthodoxy in contemporary Germany whose specific purpose was to destroy the fruits of another emancipation, although the Jews, unlike the blacks, had not been slaves. Anglo-Saxondom, therefore, reinforced the opposition of the white church to black gains in the troubled and volatile society of the post-bellum American south. Science as well as scripture, in a rare coincidence of ideas, decreed the submission of the children of Ham to the children of Japheth. It was a subject which flourished in the churches of Protestant Christianity, including their social gospel preachers and leaders. In 1902, a leading "anti-Negro propagandist" and "flaming apostle of Anglo-Saxonism," Thomas Dixon, a Baptist minister in North Carolina, published a highly successful racist drama entitled *The Leopard's Spots* in which a fictional southern pastor declined an invitation to a northern church in order "to maintain the racial absolutism of the Anglo-Saxon in the South."[66]

In Canada, during the same era, the Anglo-Saxon race myth flourished in Protestant Christianity, affecting its social gospel. Thus, in an early study of the immigration question, J. S. Woodsworth, a Methodist minister who admired Rauschenbusch and was the founder of Canadian socialism, as well as one of the greatest figures in Canadian parliamentary history, wrote:

America is not American. Canada will not remain Canadian. During the first half of the past century there came to be a fairly well-defined American type – that is, the true American had certain distinctive physical, mental and social characteristics. But so great has been the alien immigration that it is a question whether the old American type will predominate ... If the

Slavic or Latin elements predominate, what will it become? We in Canada are at the beginning of the process, and can only speculate as to the result. It is conceivable that the various races coming to us might remain absolutely distinct ... The presence of incompatible elements changes the entire social and political life of a country; it is a fatal barrier to the highest national life.[67]

Needless to say, these views were far from unique. In 1910, S. D. Chown, another Canadian Methodist minister with profound social gospel sympathies and one of the founding fathers of the United Church of Canada, reacted almost melodramatically to the latest tide of non-Anglo-Saxon immigrants: "The question of questions is which shall prevail: the ideas of Southern Europe, or the noblest conceptions of Anglo-Saxondom? 'Shall the hordes of Southern Europe overrun our country as the Huns and Vandals did the Roman Empire?'"[68] The alarm expressed by Woodsworth and Chown was a sign that, even before the First World War, English Protestant Canada was losing its confidence in the course of Anglo-Saxon historic destiny. Instead of the Anglo-Saxons crowding out the "lesser" peoples, the "lesser" peoples were now in danger of crowding out the Anglo-Saxons. Cassandra's voice, with its cry of racial doom, had not been heard in the realms of Anglo-Saxondom for the last time.

"FINIS AMERICAE,"
"FINIS BRITANNIAE"

As long as the Anglo-Saxon myth was wedded to the spirit of Anglo-American triumphalism, which is to say as long as the goddess of fortune continued to smile on the great Anglo-Saxon nations and the Pax Anglo-Americana, its more malevolent aspects were couched in relatively mild terms. Strong, as we have seen, was a man of charitable instincts who disliked the idea of a war of racial extermination. When, however, the shadows began to descend on the Anglo-Saxon hegemony during the twentieth century, and the glowing expectations of the nineteenth-century apostles of Anglo-Saxon imperialism and expansionism were rudely disappointed, the myth revealed a different face. For example, the New York patrician Madison Grant (1865–1937) found the spectacle of an "increasing number of the weak, the broken and the mentally crippled of all races drawn from the lowest stratum of the Mediterranean basin and the Balkans, together with hordes of the wretched, submerged populations of the Polish ghettos" crowding the sidewalks of Boston, Philadelphia, and New York after the turn of the century more than obnoxious.[69]

In his opinion, the tides of alien immigration from a troubled Europe were sweeping America toward racial ruin. Must not a melting pot "allowed to boil without control" result in the annihilation of the native American or "Nordic man" (a term that Grant preferred to Anglo-Saxon), of whom, of course, the author of *The Passing of the Great Race* regarded himself as a prime specimen?[70] Since, in his view, the original Aryan race had vanished in the mists of primordial time,[71] it was more accurate to speak in the modern era of the Nordic race, or the "white man par excellence," as the "great race." Tragically, however, the great race, like its remote Aryan ancestor, and even like Cro-Magnon man, the "Nordic of his day," was now passing.[72].

Grant could not resist the temptation to deck these themes in religious dress. Christ, the greatest member of the great race, was blond and Nordic like the Olympian gods; suggestively, the blond Nordic (Anglo-Saxon) Jesus was crucified between two "brunet" thieves.[73] Could it have been otherwise in an America suddenly fearful of the "dark stranger" – the Jew, the Balkan, the black – whose very presence undoubtedly stirred subconscious mythical feelings of an underworld of evil that Christ, the conqueror of darkness, came to destroy? Belief in nativism, that peculiar reflex-action of an Anglo-Saxon society seized by irrational fears of revolution during a post-war depression and a mounting social crisis led to the victimizing of Jews and blacks alike, especially in the deep south. Soon, with support from the auto magnate Henry Ford, it would lead to widespread antisemitism.[74]

The parallels between the thinking of Grant and Count Gobineau are noteworthy. Civilization was again portrayed as suspended over a racial abyss from which nothing could save it. As civilization only flourishes when the elite remain on the seats of power, the decline and fall of the Anglo-Saxons in twentieth-century America was identified by men such as Grant with the decline and fall of civilization in its entirety, for which, naturally, Jews, Latins, and Slavs were to blame. Like Gobineau, Grant was motivated by *ressentiment*, which he expressed in racist terms. Both were members of dying castes in their own societies who turned to racist ideologies for solace. In the mind of the American nativist and racist (who was by no means alone in his views),[75] warfare and miscegenation were responsible for the depletion of the Nordic race since, as nature's warrior, Nordic man is the natural victim of war. Ironically, and contrary to the faith of the Social Darwinians, the unfit rather than the fit were the main survivors of the 1914–18 débacle, causing evolution to turn downward.

Social Darwinism was congenial as long as history confirmed racist beliefs and the superior race seemed to be winning the struggle, but less congenial when nature, or what Ernst Nolte has called the "world's primeval brutality,"[76] turned on the wrong victims, as it clearly did during the First World War. For those who held such views, once confidence in nature and history was shattered, but convictions of racial superiority were not, the only recourse was to rail against everyone and everything, sounding the death knell of the entire social order. "Finis Americae," Grant cried at the beginning of his lament, exactly as Wilhelm Marr, the "patriarch of antisemitism" had once cried "Finis Germaniae" at the end of his lament on the impending victory of Judaism over Germanism![77]

This extraordinary and melodramatic pessimism was echoed more recently in post-imperial Britain, where the immigration of racial aliens is still an intensely emotional issue, by the ex-Tory parliamentarian and classical scholar John Enoch Powell (1912–). Following an increase in the number of coloured ex-imperial subjects entering the British isles from the Commonwealth during the 1960s, Powell, in a vein reminiscent of Gobineau in racially-mixed Paris a century earlier, suggested that civilization – in this case, British civilization – was in mortal peril: "In all of its history our nation has never known a greater danger."[78] The huge numbers of West Indians, Africans, and Asians then turning Wolverhampton, Smethwick, and Birmingham into "alien" territories would surely undermine and finally destroy the singular fabric of English freedom if their invasion remained unchecked.[79]

Although Powell repeatedly denied that his antagonism to coloured immigrants was influenced by biological race doctrines, insisting that only a profound concern for the preservation of British culture and the genius of Britain's political institutions caused him to speak as he did, the Anglo-Saxon racial mythology can still be found in his writings. To be English is to be born and bred English, but birth alone is insufficient since racial aliens, even if born in England, do not thereby become Englishmen, nor can they. In law, of course, the West Indian or Asian may become a citizen of the United Kingdom; however, legality is not nature and cannot bestow natural rights. Consequently, according to Powell, "in fact" such an individual "is a West Indian or Asian still."[80] The true Englishman is rooted in the unbroken life of England and possesses authentic English instincts that for generation after generation have existed on English soil. Small numbers of alien elements can be assimilated successfully only over an extended period of time. The gates had to be closed. While Powell did not utter the words "Finis Britanniae" at the conclusion of his speeches, they nevertheless resound with this message. They were motivated by fear, and thus, although milder in character, finish on the same note as the prognostications of Madison Grant. This fear, moreover, still reverberates as a discordant chord in British politics; while Powell has himself retired from the parliamentary stage, Anglo-Saxon nativism has by no means disappeared, either in Britain or elsewhere.[81] Its demon is alive and well.

CHAPTER FIVE

The Afrikaner Christ

While there are obvious differences between German and South African history, as well as between Lutheran and Calvinist Protestantism, there are also several striking parallels that help explain why racism captured so many theological and political hostages in both nations. First, the patterns of sacred history (or civil religion) have been much the same in both countries: the holy nation or chosen people, defeated by its pagan enemies, dreamt of vindication at the hands of God through the overthrow of the existing situation – in the case of Germany, the Weimar Republic, in the case of South Africa, the British dominion – and the establishment of a more suitable political order.[1] Second, the patterns of contemporary theology are similar: the word of God has supplied the creation with a clear and definite structure for the proper organization of human life, and fidelity to God's word requires a careful and constant observation of the heavenly decrees. Third, the patterns of romantic philosophy are similar: largely because of Fichte and his fellow nationalists, for the Afrikaners as well as the Germans, the nation and its racial roots became part of the divine order and hallowed objects in their own right. Fourth, the patterns of racial legislation have been much the same: the racist state, once it had achieved power – seemingly providentially – moved swiftly to separate the races by Draconian laws, thereby inaugurating an entirely new era.

Of course, there are also significant contrasts between the two racist societies. The Aryan myth, so central and powerful in German racism, apparently played a much less significant role in the Afrikaner myth, and biological race doctrines, the scientific extension of the Aryan myth, while not unknown, were not as important in South Africa.[2] Although the intellectual roots of Afrikaner ideology are certainly European, apartheid itself, in both theory and practice, has a strongly indigenous character.

The myth of Afrikanerdom, the national and racial myth of the Dutch-descended South Africans, was born out of the peculiar experiences of the Afrikaners at the hands of their real and imagined oppressors during the nineteenth and twentieth centuries. An intensely devout society which drew its paradigms from a literalistic reading of the biblical scriptures, especially the Old Testament, the "puritans" of Africa, as W. A. de Klerk has described them,[3] interpreted their history as the tale of a latter-day Israel, replete with extraordinary analogies to the ancient narrative.

As Israel was liberated from bondage to the Egyptians, so Afrikanerdom, the latter-day Israel, was liberated from bondage to the modern Egyptians, i.e., the British; as Israel was led into the wilderness under divine guidance in search of the promised land, so Afrikanerdom was divinely guided on the Great Trek in search of its own Canaan, where, like its ancient counterpart, it was forced to battle the Canaanites, i.e., the Zulus; as Israel established a covenant with God at Mount Sinai, so Afrikanerdom established a covenant with God at Blood River (1838) following a miraculous victory; as the twin kingdoms of Judah and Israel finally fell victim to the Babylonians and Assyrians and suffered exile, so the twin republics of the Transvaal (South African Republic) and the Orange Free State finally fell victim to the modern Babylonians and Assyrians, i.e., the British once again (the Anglo-Boer War), and suffered exile, figuratively speaking; as the Israelites were finally enabled by divine decree to return from exile to the land given to their fathers, so the Afrikaner exiles were enabled by divine decree to return to the land given to *their* fathers, a return symbolized by the victory of the National Party in 1948 and the inauguration of the Afrikaner Republic in 1961 (although it was not officially so designated); as Israel rebuilt the temple and re-established the cult of its God, so the South Africans rebuilt, figuratively, the temple of Afrikanerdom and re-established the cult of *its* God, insofar as this was possible in the society that the founding fathers of the Afrikaner Republic inherited from their British predecessors.[4]

Moreover, throughout this interpretation of South African history ran the biblical theme of righteous and redemptive suffering: the Lord chastens whom he loves.[5] There can be no doubt that, through their preachers, poets, and political tractarians, the Afrikaners knew exactly who they were and why history took the form that it did. The blueprint was plainly visible in the Bible, at least to Calvinist eyes.

Foremost among the myth-makers, according to Irving Hexham, was the poet Totius (J. D. du Toit), the chronicler of Afrikaner torment during the turmoil of the war against Britain and its aftermath.[6] While the agony he described was genuine – concentration camps, a new feature of twentieth-century warfare, had been established and many Boer women and children died as a consequence of the harsh conditions of their imprisonment – it was tempting to exaggerate it by reading it back into history and raising it to cosmic proportions:

A voice is heard in Rama,
wailing and loud lamentations,
Rachel, the mother of Israel, over
her children – they are no more!

So groaned Rachel's ghost ...
But see, today's Rachels,
living Rachels, who weep
at endless children's graves.

A voice is heard all over,
weeping and wailing bitterly;
Rachel, suffering Mother, weeps over
her children – they are no more.[7]

Thus, Hexham points out, Totius fused the suffering Israelites, the massacre of the innocents in the New Testament, and the suffering of the Afrikaners and their dead children in the recent struggle with imperialism.[8] Ingeniously, Totius also connected the latter with the suffering servant theme of both Testaments and with the Christ who, in his torment and death, bore the sins of the world.

In this manner, the vicissitudes and tragedies of the defeated and tortured nation, the Afrikaner *volk*, were fitted into a divine schema and endowed with eternal significance.[9] Part of the significance of this vision was its emphasis on the special vocation, and hence separate existence, of the Afrikaner community as distinct from the alien English and black communities – the twin forces of oppression and barbarism. Other writers of the post-war generation also began to regard separation as a sacred duty and anything that threatened the separateness of the Afrikaners as demonic.[10] In their polemic against British imperialism, for example, an element of antisemitism, unusual for Calvinists, appears because of the popular identification of imperialism with capitalism and capitalism with Jewish bankers and industrialists, a view almost certainly imported from Europe, and later reinforced by the arrival of Jewish refugees from Nazi

Germany. Afrikaner journalism sometimes featured the gross "Hoggenheimer" figure, at once English and Jewish, who sought to exploit the virtuous Afrikaners.[11] Antisemitism, however, never became a major motif in Afrikaner racism, whereas anti-black feeling assumed an increasingly important role. The British presence, linked with political egalitarianism and black emancipation in the Afrikaner mind, thus appeared even more demonic.[12] Black Africans were symbols of chaos – a "chaos poised to destroy order and plunge Africa back into its long centuries of darkness"[13] – and terrifying objects. It was therefore a necessary corollary of the divine calling to keep them isolated, however great the practical difficulties.

KUYPER AND NEO-CALVINISM

Calvinist Christianity played a profound role in the Afrikaner construction of reality from the beginning. Hence, it is necessary to examine briefly the nature of Calvinism itself – not merely the simple Calvinism of the Boer republics but the more sophisticated neo-Calvinism which the architects of apartheid imported from the Netherlands in the twentieth century – to understand fully the worldview of the Afrikaners. To some extent, John Calvin's theology supplied the basis for its subsequent racial elaborations, although nothing could have been further from the reformer's intentions. Double-predestination, as Simar pointed out, could be twisted easily in a racist direction, especially after later orthodox Calvinism became infused with a "mystical Platonism" that transformed the elect and the reprobate into those "good by nature" and "evil by nature."[14] When combined with classical white/black dualism and compounded by the notorious Calvinist failings of self-righteousness and, on occasion, hardness-of-heart, the potential for a full-fledged racism existed in the Dutch colonies long before the development of the racial politics of contemporary South Africa. That does not mean, of course, that the early Dutch settlers in the Cape were conscious racists, but only that the possibility of a racist ideology was embedded in the kind of Calvinist piety that the white Europeans planted on African soil.

This racist possibility, however, was realized through both the events of Afrikaner history and the fresh currents of neo-Calvinism that a new generation of post-war twentieth-century theologians absorbed at the Free University of Amsterdam – the Mecca, as Dunbar Moodie describes it, for students from the more conservative segments of the reformed community, both at home and abroad[15] – where the ideas of Abraham Kuyper (1837–1920), a Dutch theologian and politician, were in full flower. Kuyper, although scarcely a racist himself (in spite of some passages in his lectures on Calvinism that might be regarded in this light today),[16] and strongly opposed to most of the romantic and nationalistic concepts that were destined to become part of Afrikaner as well as European racism,[17] nevertheless became one of the intellectual godparents of a racist system in a country in which he did not live and whose peculiar ethos he probably never fully understood. A figure of considerable stature, Kuyper served as prime minister of the Netherlands from 1901 to 1905, ruling according to Calvinist principles. This supplied a model for a similar application of theology to politics in the South African situation on the part of his disciples.

Like all Calvinists, Kuyper's starting point was the sovereignty of God – "the Sovereignty of the Triune God over the whole Cosmos"[18] – that great theme that reverberates throughout Calvin's *Institutes of the Christian Religion*. Sovereignty, however, or the reign of God over the created order, acquired a different significance in Kuyper's theology than in Calvin's. Kuyper did not regard this as a liability since, in his eyes, Calvinism was a total "life-system" as well as the highest possible expression of Christianity, and total life-systems have their own inner laws of development.[19] One of these laws seems to have entailed the notion that the highest form of religion, i.e., Calvinist Christianity, and the highest kind of human being on the creaturely scale, i.e., the white race (*not* the children of Ham) belonged naturally together.[20] Against the relativists of his day, and the rationalistic influences that had dominated the Netherlands since the time of Napoleon, Kuyper, following another Dutch neo-Calvinist, Guillaume Groen van Prinsterer (1801–76), asserted a higher sovereignty than the sovereignty of reason and worked out its theological and social implications in a way that, as his critics have noticed,[21] resembled Luther's old orders of creation and the modern German *Theologie der Schöpfungsordnungen* theologians more than it resembled Calvin.

Sphere sovereignty, or "sovereignty in the individual social spheres," implied that the Creator had divided life into a series of compartments – family, business, science, art, etc. – and that these compartments, by virtue of the divine word, possessed an integrity and structural unity that must not be interfered with by any purely human institution.[22] Having "nothing above themselves but God," the spheres were subject to no laws except the divinely ordained laws of their own organic natures, which must be recognized and honoured by the state.[23] The state itself, interestingly, was not regarded by Kuyper as a legitimate sphere in its own right, but as a mechanical necessity: a concession to the Fall and hence inferior to such organic institutions as the family, with its blood ties, and other natural and instinctive relationships. Peoples and nations, which are not the same as governments and political systems, belong in the latter category, although they also seem to have originated as a result of human sinfulness and the disintegration of primordial human unity at the tower of Babel.[24] According to Herman Dooyeweerd, an element of inconsistency coloured Kuyper's thought at this point; slipping away from his own biblical principles, he occasionally designated the nation as a separate sovereign sphere embracing all other social spheres and leading to dangerous ideas such as the notion of "organic franchise."[25] Here, in spite of his strongly stated antagonism to the German "historico-pantheistic" school, Kuyper descended into popular romanticism, including the conviction that each nation has a distinctive national (and ultimately racial) folk-spirit. Indirectly, if not directly, he was influenced by Fichte and the other German romantic philosophers of the preceding age.

This Germanic strain was mostly filtered through Kuyper's predecessor Groen van Prinsterer and the latter's German mentor Friedrich Julius Stahl (1802–61).[26] Stahl was the decisive figure, and, if Herbert Marcuse is correct, an important voice in both the romantic reaction against rationalism and the defence of authoritarian and organic doctrines of the rights of the *Volk*.[27] "Only the *Volk*," Stahl declared, "possesses the unity of *Lebensanschauung* [an outlook on life] and the germ of creative production."[28] This Fichtean sentiment cannot have been accidental. As Fichte was one of the main founders of German nationalism, as well as its first true theoretician, there can be no doubt that his shadow fell over Stahl as well as others of Stahl's generation. The younger philosopher (Stahl was twelve years old when Fichte died), being a converted Jew, sought to attach his historical romanticism to a less mystical, more Hebraic understanding of Christianity, reconciling immanence and transcendence. For him, the nation-creating spirit of history was under the jurisdiction of the transcendent God of the Bible whose moral laws (ten commandments) served as a source of restraint on any idolatrous and dangerous tendencies.[29] It was this combination of the historical and the transhistorical that impressed Groen van Prinsterer, and which he passed on to Kuyper. The neo-Calvinist idea of a state along *"historical-national"* lines thoroughly suited the Dutch national character.[30] Hence, the anti-revolutionary party that Groen van Prinsterer founded, and that Kuyper eventully led to power, was suckled on the milk of the German romantic revival as well as that of the Swiss Reformation.

In South Africa, as de Klerk has noted, this aspect of Kuyper's thought was adopted with a special fervour.[31] Has not God created the nations, endowing each one with its own peculiar character? A. P. Treurnicht, for example, the editor of the Nederduits Gereformeerde Church weekly *Die Klerkbode*, viewed the nation as a wholly autonomous sphere of life in far less ambiguous terms than Kuyper, arguing, in a manner reminiscent of the German Christian theologians of the Third Reich, that its inner laws command absolute obedience.[32] Justice, Treurnicht maintained, "is best attained by way of differentiation or separate development." Justice is a "holy partiality" for what is different rather than what is similar among the peoples: justice entails respect for the Creator, which means respect for the Creator's laws, which means respect for one's own "particular character," which means respect (and support) for a political policy that promotes the separation of the various nations with their various particular characters.[33] This view, elaborated by Afrikaner theologians, supplied Afrikaner religious and political orthodoxy with its fundamental credo. However, the link with Fichte was not merely through Dutch neo-Calvinism, or through the distillation of its romantic components. It was also far more direct.

FICHTE AND THE AFRIKANERS

For pre-World War II Afrikaner intellectuals interested in political philosophy rather than theology, Germany rather than the Netherlands seemed an appropriate destination for post-graduate studies. Perhaps because their sojourn coincided with a new rise of German nationalism, a significant number fell under the spell of Fichte's *Addresses to the German Nation*. (It was Fichte's praise of the Germans that, as we have noted, established a distant link with Tacitus.) One of them, Nicolaas Diederichs, later a professor, a Nationalist cabinet minister, and state president of the republic, published a highly influential study of nationalism in 1936 that effectively wedded a number of Fichtean themes to the Afrikaner consciousness.[34] Nations, he informed his readers, rather than individuals, are paramount; indeed, "the individual in itself is nothing, but only becomes itself in the nation as the highest [human] community."[35] Contrary to the rationalistic doctrines of the liberal and revolutionary tradition with their necessary individualism, our essential humanity comes from the nation to which we belong and which endows our lives with spiritual meaning. Furthermore, Diederichs declared, certain nations have been assigned special tasks by divine providence, and must accept and fulfil these tasks for the sake of the creation as a whole; otherwise, the Creator's will cannot be fulfilled.[36]

Fichte's Germany had a special vocation; Diederich's Afrikanerdom, which, like Fichte's Germany, had not yet achieved its proper political incarnation, also had a special vocation. Fichte's Germans, alone among contemporary Europeans, had remained in close communion with the spiritual ground of their being; Diederichs' Afrikaners had also remained in close communion with the spiritual ground of their being – in this case with the Calvinist rather than the more mystical Lutheran God. For Fichte and the other German romantic nationalists of his day, the German language had a spiritual as well as a racial significance: it was closer to the soil than the neo-Latin languages, and consequently more authentic and vital. For the Fichtean Afrikaners, such as D. F. Malan (later the first Nationalist prime minister), Afrikaans was also a "living" language "born from the soil of the People's heart" and the unique vehicle of the Afrikaner genius.[37] Like the neo-Latin French in the Napoleonic era, the South African English were regarded as inferior, either because they, unlike the Afrikaners, did not constitute a "nation" in South Africa,[38] or because their values, including their religious values, were tainted with individualism, liberalism, and modernity. The racist elements always implicit in any form of Fichtean nationalism (despite the fact that Diederichs himself repudiated racial definitions of nationality in his book) were developed in subsequent versions of the theory, notably by H. G. Stoker.[39]

Hendrik Verwoerd, the third Nationalist prime minister and mastermind of apartheid, does not seem, if Colin Legum is correct, to have been a racist in at least the narrow scientific or biological understanding of the term, nor did he believe in more old-fashioned notions of white supremacy (*baasskap*).[40] On the other hand, this "Afrikaner of Afrikaners"[41] (in spite of his Dutch birth) was certainly a strong neo-Fichtean, and wholly committed to the realization of the most radical ideals of a nationalism that stressed the spiritual, cultural, and physical separation of one racial group from another. At Blood River, for example, one of the sacred sites of Afrikaner civil religion, he invoked the memory of the Voortrekkers who struggled to preserve the "purity of the blood of the nation" and inveighed against the "world spirit" of modern liberalism which threatened to engulf not merely the Afrikaner nation but the whole of white civilization, ending in the disintegration, and indeed the final destruction, of the white race itself.[42] Thus Fichte inveighed against the world spirit of his age, defending the purity of German blood and German civilization, both of which in his eyes were threatened with disintegration and

destruction. In true romantic style, Verwoerd was passionately attached to geography, believing that the very soil of the nation was
the gift of God to the elect people: "We shall keep on fighting for
the survival of the white man at the southern tip of Africa and the
religion which has been given to him to spread there ... We shall
fight for our existence and the world must know it. We cannot do
otherwise. Like Luther during the Reformation we are standing with
our backs to the wall. We are not fighting for money or possessions.
We are fighting for the life of our people."[43]

These words were uttered in 1958, when the Nationalists were
safely in power, but their mood was similar to that of Fichte's *Addresses*
in 1807, when the Prussians had their backs to the wall in French-
occupied Berlin. Was the invocation of Luther merely coincidental?
Verwoerd had studied in Germany in his youth, spending a term
each at the universities of Hamburg, Leipzig, and Berlin, and would
have had such analogies readily available. All his life he devoted
his not inconsiderable talents solely to the survival and hegemony
of the Afrikaners and their children; Afrikanerdom was his paramount
value.

The races, according to a parable in Verwoerd's 1956 speech dealing
with governmental plans for the development of black territories,
are like trees. Hence, they must grow apart: each tree has its distinctive
roots in the deep soil of its own proper spirituality, and each must
grow as its own organic nature dictates. What is suitable for whites
is not suitable for blacks, and *vice versa* (whites rather than just
Afrikaners because the future prime minister, for all of his Afrikaner
nationalism and fanatical republicanism, wished to enlist the English
on his side in the larger racial struggle for white "civilization" on a
black continent once Afrikaner dominance had been secured, and
British institutions had been crushed and replaced with Afrikaner
institutions). The white tree is already very large in size and laden
with marvellous fruits, but the black tree is only now being planted
and has yet to grow. If the blacks wish to emulate the whites, they
must not gaze with jealous eyes at their neighbour's garden; rather,
they must tend their own garden, and perhaps some day (but not
too soon) their tree might become large in size as well, bearing its
own (but obviously quite different) fruit. Some day, but, of course,
not for an extremely long time, and not without the constant su-
pervision of the white gardeners whose services, one surmises, will
always be necessary since – although Verwoerd did not say so –
however tall the black tree grows, the white tree will always be taller
and more luxuriant, having been planted so much sooner. In any

case, the two sets of gardeners must never make the mistake of fighting over their respective gardens, or both will be destroyed.[44]

The striking and highly revealing parable describes the core of apartheid in a simple pictorial fashion, and exposes unwittingly the full romantic flavour of the doctrine's underlying ideological assumptions. The organic metaphor, the conviction that diversity is richer and more interesting than uniformity, the exaltation of the particular over the general, the implied superiority of the older and taller tree with the greater fruit, and even the religious mantle that the Afrikaner statesman was fond of wrapping around his public utterances might have been taken directly from Fichte, with only a few adaptations to the South African situation. "Spiritual nature," Fichte had declared, "was able to present the essence of humanity in extremely diverse gradations in individuals and individuality as a whole, in peoples. Only when each people, left to itself, develops and forms itself in accordance with its own peculiar quality, and only when in every people each individual develops himself in accordance with that common quality, as well as in accordance with his own peculiar quality – then, and then only, does the manifestation of divinity appear in its true mirror as it ought to be."[45] Fichte, however, was not a Calvinist. Then, and then only, a Calvinist such as Verwoerd was more likely to add, will God be pleased and the divine name glorified. The implication of Verwoerd's Fichtean speech, delivered before an audience of "Bantu" chiefs, was that the peculiar quality of the African tribes must never tempt them to claim equal rights with non-Africans. The ersatz-European is an offence against both nature and God. A tribal people must remain true to its tribalism at all costs, or evil will ensue.

Apartheid, therefore, has Fichtean as well as Calvinist roots: the concept is a compound of a racialized neo-Fichteanism and a racialized neo-Calvinism. As such, it represents no ordinary system of institutionalized racism but a "theologized nationalism" arising out of a quasi-religious historical myth in which God, blood, race, nation, and soil are tightly intertwined.[46] This synthesis makes it truly formidable, enabling its defenders to resist a host of enemies. Moreover, the Afrikaner mind, which regards itself above all as a Christian mind, can remain unruffled by the fall of the Aryan myth since, to all intents and purposes, it never drew its basic sustenance from European-style biological doctrines in the first place (although Verwoerd was tainted with antisemitism in spite of his dislike of National Socialism).[47] Not the theories of Knox, Gobineau, Chamberlain, *et al.*, nor the racial science of the Social Darwinists, but the interplay of other symbols and ideas in the crucible of Afrikaner history produced what, in spite of the religious and philosophical antecedents we have traced, is mostly *sui generis* in Afrikaner society.

For this reason, we do not encounter the Aryan Christ of the German Christians – at least not typically, unless the secret papers of the Broederbond tell a different tale[48] – the deified Aryan, or the more extreme features of the infected Christianity of the European milieu during the late nineteenth and early twentieth centuries. Nevertheless, we can speak, albeit in a somewhat altered context, of the "racist captivity" of the Afrikaner theologians as we spoke of the racist captivity of the German Christian theologians, and of the manner in which this captivity has distorted their understanding of the Christian faith. As Germanic assumptions about God, blood, race, and nation coloured German theology and biblical exegesis during the Third Reich, Afrikaner assumptions about the same subjects have coloured Afrikaner (Calvinist) theology and biblical exegesis until the present day. Rather than the separation of the Jews from German society, however, the separation of the blacks from white society is the underlying hermeneutical principle. Like the Aryan laws in Germany, apartheid in South Africa had, and still has, its Christian apologists as well as its Christian foes.

SCRIPTURAL TEXTS

Following the master's example, Calvinist theologians have always followed the Bible closely, treating the text with the utmost seriousness. Consequently, it is scarcely surprising to find the South African disciples of Calvin true to tradition in this respect. Since Calvin, unlike Luther, emphasized the unity of scripture as a whole, regarding the Old Testament as the voice of divine revelation on a more or less equal basis with the New Testament, it was natural for his religious heirs to attach a profound and even literal significance to those biblical passages that seemed to bear directly on their historical, social, and personal experience. Providence has always been a great Calvinist theme, and Calvin's God is unceasingly active in human affairs from his lofty throne in the heavens. Who, then, can blame the puritans in Africa if they were attracted to certain portions of the holy text that reassured them of an invisible guiding hand in the midst of their trials and troubles? The dialectic between the written word and the existential situation forged the mighty frame of Afrikaner sacred history, and, with a little exercise of the imagination, these passages could be read in support of its central assumptions, including the notion of white/black separation and its attendant dualism. Three Old Testament passages in particular –

Genesis 1: 28, Genesis 11: 1–9, and Deuteronomy 32: 8–9 – with two New Testament passages – Acts 2: 5–11 and Acts 17: 26 – have played a critical role in Afrikaner apologetics.

Curiously, however, Genesis 9: 20–8 (the myth of Ham) has not played a major part in the social theology of the South African reformed churches,[49] although, as Moodie points out, it was certainly not absent from the pre-*apartheid* strata of the Afrikaner consciousness.[50] In this respect, the Afrikaners were different from the colonial and ante-bellum Americans for whom the myth served as a religious justification for the institution of black slavery. But, in theory at least, the architects of apartheid with their Fichtean vision of different trees in separate gardens, did not intend to promote black slavery; on the contrary, Verwoerd and the Nationalists sought to convey a message of perfect justice and harmony in which the rights of blacks were actually enhanced. The myth of an accursed black race under a decree of eternal servitude could not be fitted into such a proud and beautiful scheme of things. Indeed, to have incorporated the myth of Ham into the Afrikaner blueprint for South African society would have been tantamount to admitting that the policies of the National Party rested, as liberal South Africans have always claimed, on racist foundations. Such an admission could never be made.

Douglas Bax has written an excellent account of the Afrikaner theological interpretation of the five pivotal biblical passages mentioned above,[51] and the following comments are largely derived from his critique.

1   Genesis 1:28. "And God blessed them, and God said to them, 'Be fruitful and multiply, and fill the earth and subdue it. ...'" According to the Afrikaner exegetes, this verse implies that God desires the earth to be filled with a great diversity of races and peoples. Moreover, the diversity of races and peoples implies the diversity of cultures, so that ethnic difference belongs to the very stuff of creation as well. But, as Bax demonstrates, this obviously romantic reading of the text cannot be sustained; there is simply no "cultural injunction" in the divine command as the Afrikaner theologians believe.[52] Rather, the homogeneity of those who are to multiply and fill the earth is stressed, since they are the children of the same original parents and, unlike the plants and animals, are not divided into different kinds. Moreover, the command is not really a command but a blessing. Like the old German romantic philosophers, the Afrikaner theologians have elevated the contemporary historical reality – the variety of nations, culture, and races – to an ideal status, arguing that what is both ought to be and therefore must be, and then read their argument back into creation itself.

2   Genesis 11:1–9. This is the familiar tale of the tower of Babel which, according to Bax, has been the cardinal text of apartheid theology.[53]

Now the whole earth had one language and few words. And as men migrated in the east, they found a plain in the land of Shinar and settled there. And they said to one another, "Come, let us make bricks, and burn them thoroughly." And they had brick for stone and bitumen for mortar. Then they said, "Come, let us build ourselves a city, and a tower with its top in the heavens, and let us make a name for ourselves, lest we be scattered abroad upon the face of the whole earth." And the Lord came down to see the city and the tower, which the sons of men had built. And the Lord said, "Behold, they are one people, and they have all one language; and this is only the beginning of what they will do; and nothing that they propose to do will now be impossible for them. Come, let us go down, and there confuse their language, that they may not understand one another's speech." So the Lord scattered them abroad from there over the face of all the earth, and they left off building the city. Therefore its name was called Babel, because there the Lord confused the language of all the earth; and from there the Lord scattered them abroad over the face of all the earth.

According to the Afrikaner exegetes, this tale signifies that in constructing the great city and great tower on the plain – in other words, a concentrated and unified society – humankind deliberately defied the earlier commandment to fill the earth with a huge diversity of peoples, races, and cultures. As a result, God reasserted the original command by casting down the proud "humanistic" tower and making these human divisions deeper and more ingrained than ever. Not only is this interpretation wholly contrary to the general body of non-Afrikaner scriptural understanding, but it bedevils the entire subject by confusing the unity (linguistic and otherwise) that humankind already possessed with the pride that caused the human race to use this unity in order to build a civilization mighty enough to overcome the "threat of finitude, dispersion and insignificance in the face of the vast and mysterious world."[54] In fact, one might argue that the very attempt of the Afrikaners to purchase their security in the face of this threat through the proud tower of apartheid is a striking example of the real meaning of this Genesis parable. One might also argue that only a fatal combination of fear and hubris could prevent the same Afrikaners from discerning the "entirely fictitious" character of the notion that human unity is intrinsically sinful and that the corresponding notion that humanity is divisible into separate national states with discrete linguistic and racial qualities owes more to an old-fashioned romanticism that "gives rise to the delusions of nationalism, racialism, and tribalism" than it does to the Bible.[55] Once again, we are presented with evidence that the ghost of Fichte, as well as the ghost of Calvin, haunts the sacred precincts of Afrikaner theology.

3   Deuteronomy 32:8–9. "When the Most High gave to the nations their inheritance, when he separated the sons of men, he fixed the bounds of the peoples according to the number of the sons of God. For the Lord's portion is his people, Jacob his allotted heritage." According to the Afrikaner exegetes, this passage endorses the principle of territorial separation between national and racial groups since God has assigned each to its own geographical space. Non-Afrikaner exegesis, however, favours the view that numerical size rather than geographical boundary is the correct subject of the divine fiat in this mythological portrait of the origins of the kingdoms of the world. To each of the seventy "sons of God" (angelic beings), a pagan nation was assigned as a kind of heavenly trusteeship, whereas Israel was to be ruled directly from the throne of the "Most High." It is absurd, therefore, to apply this text to the modern South African political and racial situation, especially to the establishment of black homelands in order to preserve the so-called natural integrity of the white community. Moreover, the concept of one nation/one race/one territory is itself of romantic derivation and completely remote from the configurations of the ancient near east.

4   Acts 2:5–11. The tale of Pentecost:

Now there were dwelling in Jerusalem Jews, devout men from every nation under heaven. And at this sound the multitude came together, and they were bewildered, because each one heard them speaking in his own language. And they were amazed and wondered, saying, "Are not all these who are speaking Galileans? And how is it that we hear, each of us in his own native language? Parthians and Medes and Elamites and residents of Mesopotamia, Judea and Cappadocia, Pontus and Asia, Phrygia and Pamphylia, Egypt and the parts of Libya belonging to Cyrene, and visitors from Rome, both Jews and proselytes, Cretans and Arabians, we hear them telling in our own tongues the mighty works of God.

According to the Afrikaner exegetes, this miraculous episode reveals that the birth of the Christian church not only did not eradicate the natural divisions – linguistic, cultural, psychological, and racial – that God had imposed on humankind at the beginning, but actually confirmed them.[56] Since, however, as Bax points out, Pentecost represents the reversal of Babel, such an interpretation is untenable.[57]

Through the miracle of the divine visitation, all human divisions are transcended in the new spiritual unity of the messianic age, which cannot be splintered into ethnic and racial factions without damaging its fundamental character. Pentecost is therefore an argument against apartheid, not an argument in its support. Furthermore, the idea of national churches as envisaged by the authors of this doctrine is another legacy of nineteenth-century romanticism in which religion and nationality were closely intertwined. This view, as we have seen, particularly in the German case, prepared the way for racist fantasies.

    5   Acts 17:26. "And he made from one every nation of men to live on all the face of the earth, having determined allotted periods and the boundaries of their habitation. ..." According to the Afrikaner exegetes, this claim from Paul's great speech in Athens is still another proof-text of the fact that both human diversity and a matching territorial separation of the diverse peoples were willed by the Creator at the hour of creation. Non-Afrikaner scholars, however, disagree, arguing that the stress in Paul's words falls on the oneness rather than the divided state of humankind, and that Paul was deliberately reminding the proud Athenians who imagined that their origins were different and more glorious from the rest of humanity of this signal truth.[58] The apostle, moreover, was probably referring to the preparation of the earth rather than the sea as a home for the human creature when he spoke of periods and boundaries;[59] he was almost certainly *not* speaking of political borders. Once again, the Afrikaner interpretation bears the marks of an ideological and doctrinaire distortion of a somewhat ambiguous fragment from the New Testament that can properly be understood only as related to an ancient context.

CHRIST THE DIVIDER

Afrikaner Christianity, with its puritan contours, is both great and tragic. It is great because it sustains the soul of a small people whose determination to survive in the presence of a hostile environment has required immense human and spiritual fortitude: a living faith. It is tragic because it is profoundly flawed and can neither diagnose nor cure its own fatal disorders. Hence, the Christ of the Afrikaners, although not an Afrikaner himself, is also a flawed and highly inadequate figure. In a sense, he *is* an Afrikaner, for, if the Afrikaner Calvinists are latter-day Hebrews, as they have traditionally seen themselves, then the original Hebrews, including Jesus, must have been proto-Afrikaners. This Christ divides rather than unites, and he earnestly desires his peoples to remain apart. "Your churches," Verwoerd replied to a group of Christian leaders who had sought his permission to hold an interracial conference in 1965, "should be able to fulfil their functions fully as other Protestant churches do, while observing the country's laws and customs as they exist."[60] Under no circumstances must members of the body of Christ of different racial extractions be allowed to share room and board together. Why should they when to be one in Christ Jesus is not a matter of the flesh. Like the German Christians, the Afrikaner theologians drew a line between the spiritual and material, or the private and public aspects of life. Redemption does not alter the structures of creation, and, to "true" Christians, the word of scripture is perfectly clear. Blacks, of course, can also be Christians, but only in their own sphere which means, naturally, in their separate homelands. Thus the puritans of Africa, like so many of their European counterparts, fell victim to the racist disease in spite of their partial immunization to its main European strains.

The ravages of this disease are no less apparent in South Africa than in Europe. After the German Third Reich, the republic designed and founded by the Afrikaner Nationalists became, and still remains, the racist state *par excellence* in the eyes of the world. Official South Africa does not see itself in this light, and its leaders angrily reject external (and internal) criticism of what they regard as a just and Christian solution of a complex human problem, but this intimate identification of apartheid with Christianity only deepens the moral offence of the situation for those who cannot accept the premises of Afrikaner faith. Even the critics, however, must acknowledge that Afrikanerdom and its religious apostles cannot be blamed exclusively for the tragedy of contemporary South Africa: other white South Africans, including a substantial section of the old British community, have yielded to their own racist instincts and voted in increasing numbers in recent elections for the National Party. Ironically, out of fear of black ascendency, the children of the former Anglo-Saxon empire have now transferred their allegiance to Verwoerd's white utopia, which, in its origins at least, was as anti-British as it was anti-black. To this degree, Anglo-Saxondom and Afrikanerdom have joined forces, and the Anglo-Saxon Christ and the Afrikaner Christ have united against the black Christ. History, I suspect, will soon decide the contest.

CHAPTER SIX

The Black Christ

History contains many strange corridors. As a young man, W. E. B. Du Bois, the most scholarly figure and gifted writer in the black nationalist movement in the United States, studied briefly in Berlin under the nationalistic German historian Heinrich von Treitschke, who, like all German nationalists, drew much of his inspiration from Fichte and his contemporaries.[1] To the extent that the youthful Du Bois was influenced by Treitschke, therefore, it is possible to claim that the remote shadow of Fichte, and, through him, the even more remote shadow of Tacitus, cast their length as far as the ghettos of black America. If such a claim is not too fanciful, the conclusion follows that all forms and expressions of nationalism in the present-day world possess a family affinity, although each has its own distinctive contours.

Certainly, the pan-Africanism of Du Bois and his successors must have been suggested in part by the pan-movements launched in Europe around the turn of the century, i.e., pan-Germanism and pan-Slavism. No one can doubt, moreover, that black nationalism, like its European counterparts, was conceived in the womb of social and political alienation. What alienation could have been more terrible than that inflicted by the trauma of a violent uprooting from the African continent followed by several generations of dehumanizing slavery and the subsequent deprivations of life at the bottom of American society? All the elements of *ressentiment* appear with iridescent clarity in the writings of black American nationalists, both past and present. Nationalism, however, is not merely a negative phenomenon: it has positive aspects as well since it overcomes factionalism and disunity by creating a higher unity that, in turn, bestows a new identity and pride on the members of the newly discovered nation. Something appears that did not exist before, and this changes everything as far as the minds and hearts of the nationalists are concerned. In both its negative and positive features, black nationalism is no exception to the other nationalisms of the age.

It is no exception in another respect as well. When the black slaves imported from Africa during the colonial era were converted to Christianity by their white masters (a conversion made easy, as James Deotis Roberts has pointed out, by the natural resemblances between native African religion with its supreme deity and lesser spirits and the monotheistic religion of the ancient Hebrews with its angels and demons that the Christian church inherited[2]), they developed a tremendous love for the biblical narrative. From this biblical-Christian mould emerged a potent imagery with existential significance for the lives of the new Christians in a new land under new and intolerable conditions. Even today, the imagery persists. The contemporary Black Muslims of America, who reject Christianity as a white slave religion, are not really true Muslims at all, if Roberts is correct, but Christian heretics who cite the Bible more frequently than the Koran, thereby demonstrating the indelible character of the scriptural imprint on the black religious consciousness.[3] Not unlike the Afrikaners of the nineteenth century, black Christians absorbed the hoary themes of bondage, suffering, exile, deliverance, providence, and promise, which they interpreted in light of their own situation. Once again, the vicissitudes of the ancient Hebrews were replayed in a modern setting, especially the tale of Moses and the flight from Egypt, since those who were slaves in America had little difficulty identifying with those who were slaves in Egypt.

Consequently, the rudiments of a black sacred history began to arise prior to the birth of black nationalism proper, although without the political connotations and promethean passions of most other "elect" peoples of the day. Not until the concept of the black nation made its début on the historical scene did these latter traits appear. For the American blacks *were* a profoundly oppressed people, not a people that merely imagined itself to be oppressed (like, for example, Adolf Stöcker's so-called elect Germans), and, as the black theologians have shown, their prayers, sermons, and spirituals contain a compelling vision of a transformed social order.[4] In this respect, as their expositors claim, they undoubtedly understood the Bible far better than their white masters, making black theology far closer to the biblical message than "white" theology with its colonial ethos and its subtle commendation of slavery. Nevertheless, once a more nationalistic *Zeitgeist* prevailed, black sacred history could be interpreted in a narrow and exclusive fashion. Herein lay the danger.

MOOD EBONY

The origins of black nationalism, according to Rodney Carlisle, belong in the late ante-bellum period in American history when a circle of like-minded individuals was formed for the express purpose of promoting nationalistic ideas.[5] Not surprisingly, themes of black racial glory, including the grandeur of black civilization in former ages, the prowess of black kings, and the claim that Jesus himself must have had a black ancestor, were celebrated with gusto.[6] Africa, both real and imagined, became an object of fascination to these nineteenth-century black American men of letters, not altogether dissimilar from the nineteenth-century German romantic fascination with old Teutonic Germany; in both cases, a question of identity was involved and fact and fiction were easily mixed. This African interest was further stimulated by a number of repatriation and colonization projects that various (but not all) black nationalists promoted, especially after the foundation of the Republic of Liberia in 1847. As a type of black Zion, Africa, whether or not one really wished to return to its shores, became the consummate symbol of the black collective identity. On the basis of this symbol, what C. Eric Lincoln has described as a mystique of blackness began to develop, through which the alienated negro of America could "rediscover himself as a black man linked to the ancient civilizations of Mother Africa."[7] ("Negro", incidentally, is a white rather than a black term, and, according to modern black nationalists, ought to be rejected as an epithet of contempt.) Here, obviously, is the source of the later "black is beautiful" movement with its pulsating pride in blackness itself, and its deliberate trans-valuation of white racial values as an act of ultimate defiance:

Back beyond the world and swept by these wild, white faces of the awful dead, why will this Soul of White Folk, – this modern Prometheus, – hang bound by his own binding, tethered by a fable of the past? I hear his mighty cry reverberating through the world, "I am white!" Well and good, O Prometheus, divine thief! Is not the world wide enough for two colors, for many little shinings of the sun? Why, then, devour your own vitals if I answer even as proudly, "I am black!"[8]

"Mood ebony," to cite a once popular phrase, cast its spell over the younger generation of black intellectuals that arose in the wake of Du Bois. The conviction of black beauty – the beauty of "black eyes, black and brown, and frizzled hair curled and sleek, and skins that riot with luscious color and deep, burning blood"[9] – became a dictum of the new mentality that, in the words of Gayraud S. Wilmore, was busy "tearing itself out of the enveloping husk" of the alien white world.[10] Like most such movements, black nationalism did not speak softly or tread warily in its attempt to establish the black identity: its spokesmen grew increasingly strident in their assertions and radical in their social and political agendas. At the same time, even among the most radical nationalists, it was clear that blackness referred to more than skin colour alone: blackness was a metaphor for an entire culture in all of its manifold dimensions and their "revalorization" in a community that had survived a host of evils – slavery, miscegenation, lynching, ghettoization.[11]

Beauty, however, is an elusive concept, and the notion of black beauty, or beauty in blackness, was ambiguous from the beginning. In one sense, it *did* mean skin colour, and it *was* a conscious reversal of the more familiar aesthetics of the racial mainstream in Western society that held that white is beautiful as well as normative as far as humanity is concerned. This ambiguity found expression in the dubious thesis that the less black a person is, the less beautiful (less noble, less trustworthy, less good) that person's soul must be, thereby driving a wedge between the different segments of the black American population which, visually, are certainly not uniform. Marcus Garvey, the founder of the Universal Negro Improvement Association and perhaps the most messianic figure ever to arise in black America, was able to attack Du Bois as being far too light-skinned (on his own account, the latter's blood contained "a strain of French, a bit of Dutch, but, thank God! no 'Anglo-Saxon'"[12]) to be entrusted with the leadership of the black cause. Indeed, according to Garvey, Du Bois was really a mortal enemy of the black people since he represented an element that, hating its own negritude, was conspiring to organize a "caste aristocracy" with the "very near white" blacks dominating the authentic dark-skinned blacks (such as Garvey himself).[13] Racial purity, then, as determined by the colour criterion, became a decided ingredient in the more extreme forms of black nationalism, although Garvey's views were angrily rejected by the moderate nationalists as well as by blacks for whom "blackness" signified a cultural ethos rather than a literalistic understanding of race.[14] These denunciations, however, did not deter the black "Mussolini."[15]

Yet even the young Du Bois, like many of his contemporaries, was infected by the race doctrines that were at their zenith around the turn of the century, as his celebrated essay "The Conservation of Races" clearly demonstrates. In fact, he so thoroughly absorbed the scientific assumptions of the white intelligentsia that he called on his followers to "survey the whole question of race in human philosophy" and to design their policies and goals in light of their findings. "For it is certain that all human striving must recognize the hard limits of natural law, and that any striving, no matter how intense and earnest, which is against the constitution of the world, is vain."[16] Natural law and the constitution of the world: the decrees of such mighty forces admit of no annulment, leaving us only to recognize the "subtle, delicate and elusive" differences between the races, especially between the white and black races, that constitute the "central thought in all history."[17] Physical differences are real, according to Du Bois, but the deeper differences of mind and spirit – which, however, are related to the physical differences – are the truly important ones. Each race, consequently, is creative in its own way, including that of the negro (negro was an acceptable term to black nationalists in 1897) which, although "half-awakening in the dark forests of its African fatherland," has not yet given its full gifts to the world.[18] These gifts, when they are given, will prove to be rich and distinctive in their own right, not a "servile imitation of Anglo-Saxon culture."[19] The only question is when this will happen, which depends on the extent to which black America is prepared to embrace the vision of a "black tomorrow" and dedicate itself to its splendid realization.[20]

In this manner, much like his Anglo-Saxon counterparts, only without their self-congratulation and denigration of other races, Du Bois hinted at a racial golden age in which the "whiteness" of "Teutonic" civilization would be softened by the darker hues of the negro genius in a more harmonious and peaceful scheme of things.[21] Although his racial speculations were free from the glaring faults of the white race myths of his day (in spite of his obvious dislike of Anglo-Saxondom), they were nonetheless based on the pseudo-scientific dogmas of the white anthropologists and biologists. Only in later years, perhaps as a reaction to the racism of Nazi Germany, does he seem to have emancipated himself wholly from these earlier influences, denying (in 1938) the existence of biological races and repudiating the study of racial subjects, the inculcation of racial ideals, and the writing of racial textbooks.[22] Unfortunately, however, the seed remained.

"GOD IS A NEGRO"

In uttering these startling words, Bishop Henry M. Turner of the African Methodist Episcopal Church in the United States did not really mean what he said since he was "no stickler as to God's color, anyway," and, if he had been, he would have selected the colour blue because of the blue canopy of the skies and the blue waters of the oceans.[23] But he would not tolerate the complacent assumption of white Christians that God was made in their image and that Jesus was more or less an Anglo-Saxon and proto-(white) American. Why should blacks not have the same right as whites to believe that God is like them? Why should black Christians be coerced into believing that God is a "white-skinned, blue-eyed, straight-haired, projecting nosed, compressed lipped and finely robed *white* gentleman, sitting upon a throne somewhere in the heavens?"[24] Turner's statements, made in 1898, marked the beginning of a slowly growing "God is black" trend in black American Christianity that, for better or worse, was destined to accompany the rise of black nationalism in the twentieth century. If God is black, then Christ, the Son of God, must also be black, if not literally at least metaphorically, as Du Bois himself wrote:

> Till some dim, darker David, a-hoeing of his corn,
> And married maiden, mother of God,
> Bid the black Christ be born![25]

Neither Turner nor Du Bois, of course, intended to substitute a black racism for a white racism and reinterpret the Christian faith accordingly: they simply intended a vivid protest against the age-old colour dualism of the church in which whiteness was associated with the divine *Logos* and blackness with the powers of evil (see chapter 1). In this protest, they were fully justified. Having changed the equation, however, the two leaders of the black movement made it easy for others to do what they themselves would not, that is, to reverse its terms. When, in 1921, Garvey's protégé the Rev. George Alexander McGuire founded the African Orthodox Church as a religious offshoot of the Universal Negro Improvement Association, he immediately depicted Jesus – no longer metaphorically – as a black man and (since his church rested on Episcopalian foundations) the Virgin Mary as a black madonna.[26] The protest was no longer merely a prophetic protest against an infected white Christianity: it had acquired an ontological character of its own, with articles of faith and a reconstructed liturgy to match. McGuire's church, which still exists, was succeeded more recently by the Shrine of the Black Madonna in Detroit, Michigan, and McGuire himself was followed by the Rev. Albert B. Cleage who, in his sermons and other publications, has proclaimed the blackness of Jesus in an unmitigatedly racial sense.

The following remarkable credo appears as a preface to Cleage's book *Black Christian Nationalism*:

I Believe that human society stands under the judgment of one God, revealed to all, and known by many names. His creative power is visible in the mysteries of the universe, in the revolutionary Holy Spirit which will not long permit men to endure injustice nor to wear the shackles of bondage, in the rage of the powerless when they struggle to be free, and in the violence and conflict which even now threaten to level the hills and the mountains.

I Believe that Jesus, the Black Messiah, was a revolutionary leader, sent by God to rebuild the Black Nation Israel and to liberate Black people from powerlessness and from the oppression, brutality, and exploitation of the white gentile world.

I Believe that the revolutionary spirit of God, embodied in the Black Messiah, is born anew in each generation and that Black Christian Nationalists constitute the living remnant of God's Chosen People in this day, and are charged by Him with responsibility for the Liberation of Black People.

I Believe that both my survival and my salvation depend upon my willingness to reject INDIVIDUALISM and so I commit my life to the Liberation Struggle of Black people and accept the values, ethics, morals, and program of the Black Nation defined by that struggle, and taught by the Black Christian Nationalist Movement.[27]

A few pages later, the author of this confession declares that truth is entirely a relative affair, pertaining to the interests of a people.[28] There is no objective truth, at least none that we can know, only competing relative truths which are true only insofar as they serve our purposes and false insofar as they do not. Consequently, that "truth" becomes our authority that most truly represents our passions and concerns in a given situation at a given time. For blacks, this authoritative truth is the black liberation struggle and nothing else. If something assists this struggle, it is true, and, being true, also moral and the will of God; if something hinders this struggle, it is false, and, being false, also immoral and the will of Satan. "With this simple key to the mysteries of life both events and institutions can be judged."[29] They can indeed. Christ, according to Cleage's key, was black because he had to be black, and it is immoral and satanic to think otherwise. The ancient Hebrews – although not the modern Jews, who are not descendants of the Hebrews but of white Europeans and Asiatics who converted to Judaism a millennium ago[30] – were also black, as was their ancestor Abraham, their lawgiver Moses, and even the Canaanites and Babylonians. Not only was Israel a black nation, it was also the elect nation and thus the object of white pagan hatred and the victim of white oppression. The biblical saga reached a climax when Jesus, the black (Zealot) messiah, under divine inspiration, struggled to free the elect black nation from its white Roman oppressors, with consequences only too familiar. Crucified because he attempted to liberate the black nation, Israel, he nevertheless managed through his resurrection to resurrect his people as well, or at least to inaugurate the process of their eventual liberation.[31] This, of course, would be the real resurrection. Unfortunately, however, the will of God at this point was frustrated by a tragic betrayal. Paul, the black Hebrew "Uncle Tom" of antiquity, turned the black religion of Christianity into a white slave religion by imposing a white theology on the followers of Jesus and thereby selling out to the Roman oppressors.[32] The church has suffered from this distortion ever since.

Today, as a result, it is imperative on the part of true Christians to purge their faith of these corrupt elements and return to the original teachings of Jesus. Like Marcion, Cleage wishes to eliminate everything that offends his sensibilities from the pages of the New Testament; unlike Marcion, his purpose is to bring the gospel in line with the Old Testament, that book of early "black power" that transcends every modern book, and which saw Jesus fulfilled as the black messiah.[33] Paul, for example, smothered the realities of black oppression by fashioning a hypocritical universal love-ethic out of the quite different "tribal ethic" that Jesus bequeathed to the black nation: "If a Black brother strikes you upon one cheek, turn to him the other cheek, because we must save every Black brother for the nation if we are to survive."[34] Fortunately, there are signs of renewal. In the Shrine of the Black Madonna, authentic Christianity has been reborn in a black Protestant Reformation, and the black nation, God's elect, has been reconstituted as a nucleus for the liberation of both America and Africa from white colonialism.

The axis of the foregoing theology, and a theme that pervades the whole of romantic nationalism, is the identification of the church with the nation so that the nation becomes the real church and the bearer of the divine self-revelation. Cleage is quite explicit about this: only a people "can feel the Holy Spirit." Individuals cannot, and only a specific people, "the remnant of the Nation Israel" (dare one say the black *Volk*?), received the Holy Spirit at Pentecost, when the Christian church was born.[35] A people, of course, is always more than a mere aggregate of individuals as far as the romantic understanding is concerned: it possesses a mental and spiritual life of its own. Salvation, moreover, is never accomplished "on a one-to-one basis without the mediation of the church as Nation."[36] Nationhood, therefore, is the nexus of the divine/human encounter, and nationality, exactly as it was for the German romantics of the nineteenth century, is a sacred feeling whose holy embers burn in the soul. This collective mystique in which patriotism and faith are fused and in which, and only in which, the individual finds his or her individuality, is absolutely paramount for Cleage.

Neither Fichte nor Schleiermacher could have made the point more vigorously. One might even speak of black "God-consciousness" since, according to Cleage, all true religion arose out of black religion with its profound spirituality; white religion, on the other hand, as exemplified by the Roman pagans, had neither sense nor knowledge of God.[37] One might also speak of a black *Wiedergeburt* (spiritual rebirth), since a racial evangelicial revival on a national scale is clearly the pietistic core of Cleage's message. Certainly, the elect blacks, like the elect Germans of an earlier era, are charged with a divinely inspired mission amid the modern pagans – the white gentile nations – and the future of history is in their hands. Fichte believed that the German nation required a new, carefully nurtured appreciation of its special genius in light of its predestined role; Cleage apparently holds the same belief about the black nation.

On the other hand, the apostle of the black messiah, in spite of his impassioned words about white bestiality – the "white man is the only animal on the face of the earth who deliberately fouls the very air he must breathe, the water he must drink, and the earth upon which he must live"[38] – does not accept the Yakub myth of the more extreme Black Muslims with its white demonology.[39] Black Christian Nationalists, we are told, do not need such a myth: "the white man for us is neither a devil nor a beast but a power-crazy individualist who can be dealt with and defeated in struggle."[40]

At this point, a small note of realism enters Cleage's declamations, including the recognition that the will to power is universal, and that blacks as well as whites can be corrupted by the same set of temptations. "We have two beasts to fight: the beast within and the beast without. To neglect one is as dangerous as to misunderstand the other."[41] Does he mean, then, that his own theology with its black sacred history and black Christ is more a tract for the times written out of a mood of "sorrow, bitterness, anger and hatred," to cite an African critic,[42] than a final and absolute statement of truth? Are all human beings of one blood and the children of a single God? If black liberation should ever be fully realized, as Cleage so fervently desires, would the black messiah lose his blackness? Can Christ be white as well as black if whites are not, as the Yakub myth asserts, the authors of all evil? Is Cleage's rejection of the latter an attempt to divert his thought from the racism to which both its rhetoric and logic so clearly point, especially his idolization of the black nation? Has he suddenly become conscious of the dangers of black racism in the extremist ideology of the Black Muslims – an ideology in which the role of primordial ancestor and noble hero is played by the black Adam and that of the anti-hero by the white fiend?

Cleage, unfortunately, does not supply his readers with sufficient evidence to permit an affirmative answer to these questions, although his views concerning the relative nature of truth support such a conclusion, and the hint of amelioration is present if the two beasts analogy is to be taken seriously. What is Cleage's *real* message? In the final analysis, it is impossible to say.

BLACK THEOLOGY

The black Christ also appears in the pages of the more academic black theologians of our time, notably the writings of James Cone which have played a pivotal role in the development of the movement and the propagation of its ideas. Like Cleage, Cone regards the struggle for black liberation as both the starting point and guiding consideration of his thought: consequently, the whole of scripture and the subsequent history of Christianity is read and interpreted accordingly. On the basis of this hermeneutical principle, Cone, like Cleage, proclaims that Jesus is black because, as a Jew, he was a member of an oppressed people and, since the victims of oppression in the modern world are invariably black, the victims of oppression in the ancient world must also have been black, if not literally, at least symbolically. "He *is* black because he *was* a Jew. The affirmation of the Black Christ can be understood when the significance of his past Jewishness is related dialectically to the significance of his present blackness."[43] Thus the cross and resurrection signify the presence of God in the midst of (black) human suffering and the conquest of the sources of this suffering, (white) human injustice. "If Jesus' presence is real and not docetic, is it not true that Christ *must* be black in order to remain faithful to the divine promise to bear the suffering of the poor?"[44] Of course, Cone adds, the time may come when it will no longer be necessary to insist on the blackness of Jesus, but, until that time comes, it is a matter of crucial importance, essential to the gospel itself, to stress this fact. Indeed, the proclamation of the black Christ is nothing less than the word of God for today; the proclamation of any other Christ falsifies the divine word and distorts the entire meaning of both the Bible and the Christian faith.

Not content with this version of Luther's "hier stehe ich," Cone refines his proclamation by insisting that Christ was black in a literal as well as in a symbolic sense, although he does not seem to use the term "literal" quite literally. "The literal significance of Jesus' blackness [means] that he *was not* white! He was a Palestinian Jew whose racial ancestry may have been partly African but definitely not European."[45] To be not white is not the same as to be black, and while Jesus (contra Chamberlain) was not European, there is no evidence to suggest that his ancestry was African. The symbolic blackness of Christ, Cone holds, arises from the manner in which God, from the beginning, has sided with the poor and marginalized (i.e., black) people of the earth throughout the terrible tale of their victimization, making black history and black humanity the receptacle of the divine self-revelation. "To say that Christ is black means that God, in his infinite wisdom and mercy, not only takes color seriously, he takes it upon himself and discloses his will to make us whole – new creatures born in the spirit of divine blackness and redeemed through the blood of the Black Christ."[46]

The black Christ, therefore, atones for the sins of the world, and the redeemed creature, in contrast to Origen's vision of the conversion of the black soul to a white and heavenly state, experiences the transformation of its sinful whiteness into a divine blackness. Since, in both cases, the colour imagery is figurative, it is clear that Cone, like Origen, does not believe that the Son of God died only for a single race. Otherwise, the black Christ would be no different from the Jupiter-Christ of the French racists who died exclusively for the Latin race. Black theology, which originated as a protest against racism, could hardly argue that not to be black (in the physical sense) is not to be redeemed, or not capable of redemption, without betraying its own first principles. Cone, especially in his more recent writings, has expressed his abhorrence of this idea, emphasizing his intrinsic universalism.[47] Nevertheless, his theological language is highly ambiguous and problematic, even on the symbolic level. Origen, too, was a universalist, but his choice of words and images was not salutary for the western religious tradition. In spite of his rejection of the more extreme manifestations of black American nationalism, and his commitment to the larger dimensions of the Christian understanding of salvation, Cone does not escape Origen's dilemma.[48] His black Christ is an antithetical figure, whose religious power depends on the contemporary black rebellion against white theology with its white Christ, white churches and white systems of social oppression; in himself, he is devoid of significance. The fact, however, that he is black allows black nationalists to use him as a racist deity, not withstanding Cone's objections, nor those of other moderate black Christians. Thus, as Rosemary Ruether has written, the black theologians constantly walk a "razor's edge between a racist message and a message that is validly prophetic."[49] I concur with this judgment.

CHAPTER SEVEN

Conclusion

In his great book of thirty-five years ago, H. Richard Niebuhr defined the "Christ of Culture" as one of the five solutions to the enduring problem of the relationship between Christianity and culture.[1] Throughout the whole of Christian history, he argued, certain Christians have instinctively sought to harmonize the central figure of their faith with the cultural world in which they lived, resulting, inevitably, in an attempt to excise "stubbornly discordant features" from the New Testament.[2] The various Christs described in the preceding pages of this study are examples of this tendency. Since, however, both nationalism and racism, the twin cultural moulds in which these five Christs have been cast, are the products of modernity, they are thoroughly modern examples that could not have been conceived in an earlier period. As such, they collectively represent extreme expressions of the Christ of culture motif and are examples of the moral and spiritual hazards that arise from too close an identification between the symbols of religion and the forms of civilization.

In itself, there is nothing wrong in the attempt of Christians with different national and racial origins to claim Christ as their own; indeed, unless the Christian saviour belongs in some sense to all Christians and all types of Christians, Christian universalism is devoid of real significance. It is legitimate, therefore, for national churches to portray Christ as a German, Latin, Anglo-Saxon, Afrikaner, or black – not to mention a score of other possibilities – *provided* both that he is not confined exclusively to any of these national and racial classifications and that the Jesus of history – a Jew of the first century – is not obscured behind the Christ of faith, so that his initial and essential Jewishness is downgraded or abolished. If these provisos are not heeded, the process of what Clark M. Williamson calls the contextualization of Christianity in a series of new cultures acquires a radically different character, leading to idolatrous results.[3] Christ, in that case, is soon transformed into a tribal deity, usually an anti-Jewish tribal deity, as menacing as any of the Ba'als of the ancient Near East. Racist ideologies are certain to promote this transformation, but, since nationalism always contains the seeds of racism, it alone can also have a similar effect, especially when its boundaries are tightly drawn.

The fact that the Jesus of history was neither an Aryan, a German, a Frenchman, an Anglo-Saxon, an Afrikaner, or a black cannot be emphasized too strongly, not only for reasons of historical accuracy but also because Christians must never be allowed to forget that the Christ in whom they believe is always *against* as well as *for* their particular cultures. To acknowledge the Jewishness of Jesus, as Williamson also points out, is to employ a potent antidote to a culture-bound Christianity, an antidote that forces modern followers of Jesus to cleave to their Jewish roots "while the fruit from Christian branches falls on Gentile soil."[4] This insight is not new. Karl Barth, in one of his post-war radio addresses, issued a warning against the cultural Protestantism that had wreaked such terrible havoc in recent European experience by reminding his listeners of the Johannine dictum: "Salvation is of the Jews!" (John 4:22). "The sun shines down," Barth declared, "not on the Egyptians and Babylonians, not on the Philistines and Moabites, not on the Greeks and Romans, not on the English nor on the Swiss, but on the chosen people of Israel, the Jews. ..."[5] One need not agree with the great theologian's peculiar and highly controversial views concerning the meaning of Jewish chosenness in order to appreciate the force of his words for a society that was more inclined to regard quite different groups as chosen and basking in the sunlight. Neither German "sacred" history, nor its French, English, American, Afrikaner, or black counterparts, ought to be considered sacred in the biblical sense; it is a profound and dangerous illusion on the part of modern nations to see themselves as part of the scriptures in this elevated fashion. When the appropriation of biblical sacred history is compounded by the possession of military and political power, as has sometimes been the case, its dangers are multiplied to a pronounced degree. Election, moreover, even in the Bible, must be regarded as an ambiguous concept, with which the children of Israel had constant difficulty. On the one hand, it represents a call to mission and service, or to be a light to the nations; on the other hand, as the prophets knew, it contains a subtle temptation to *hubris* and related sins.

These ambiguities still haunt the present age, raising the perennial problem that confronts every large and semi-homogeneous community: how its particularistic claims and universalistic ideals are to be kept in equilibrium. If the particular is exalted above the universal, something essential to civilized life is sacrificed, with destructive consequences as far as the moral well-being of the nation, race, or nation-race and its culture are concerned. If the universal is exalted above the particular, something equally essential is sacrificed and, human nature being what it is, can achieve its revenge by reappearing in an exaggerated and distorted form. One of the reasons for the rise of nationalism and racism after the eighteenth century was a legitimate romantic protest against the frequently artificial and false universalism of the Age of Reason and its facile assumptions about the rationality of both the individual and the human species. Fichte was not completely wrong when he asserted the distinctiveness of the German identity, any more than his successors (and, for that matter, his predecessors, if one recalls the late medieval *Book of a Hundred Chapters*) were completely wrong in their protest against a Latinized Christianity that had falsely universalized the configurations of Greco-Roman culture since the fall of Rome. One can appreciate the cry for an indigenous Christianity, or rather for an indigenous manifestation of the Christian faith. However, Fichte and the later neo-Fichteans invariably went too far, yielding to the promethean passions that every assertion of this kind is bound to stir and to the underlying egotism that must always be reckoned with in human affairs. This was especially true when the apostles of nationalism (and racism) concentrated on the grandeur, nobility, and beauty of their own cultures, nations, and races, fueling the fires of narcissism and its attendant perils.

No doubt, under circumstances of political, social, and cultural oppression, it is vital for an alienated and downtrodden people to rebuild its collective self-image by emphasizing everything that seems distinctive and worthwhile in its traditions and organic life, including even physical and racial attributes if these have been denigrated. Self-hatred is certainly the most debilitating of hatreds, and what is true of individuals is in this case also true of groups: unless one begins with a healthy self-love, one cannot love others, either individually or *en masse*. Hence, it was crucial for Fichte's Germans, in the context of Napoleonic imperialism, to affirm their own national genius, even if this affirmation led to some ridiculous and grossly inflated claims. Similarly, it has been crucial for American blacks, in the context of white oppression, to declare that "black is beautiful," inverting the insults of their enemies. At the same time, once these self-affirmations have been uttered and accepted, restoring the lost pride and emasculated dignity of the alienated people, to reiterate them uncritically is to risk turning them into the slogans of a new triumphalism, should the circumstances of history change.

Much of what has been depicted in the tales of our various Christs has to do with liberation, a fashionable word in modern theology: the liberation of the oppressed Germans, French, Saxons, Afrikaners, blacks. But, in the past, our study suggests, the rhetoric of liberation, when magnified by too much self-love, tended to become a different kind of rhetoric entirely once the Germans, French, Saxons and Afrikaners found themselves in positions of power and ascendancy over others. If, in the future, this pattern is repeated, will the blacks prove an exception? History, the late Reinhold Niebuhr is alleged to have said, will confirm how readily the oppressed of yesterday and today can turn into the oppressors of tomorrow, unless they are careful to heed the lessons of the past.[6] History, at least in the case of the Afrikaners, has already established the truth of this observation.

The racial Christs of the cultures we have examined are probably not the last such configurations that the Christian world will produce, since Christians, like everyone else, find it difficult to abjure old follies. Once the Jewishness of Jesus has been diluted, moreover, Christianity is easily captured by nationalism and racism, and, once captured, is not so easily rescued from their snares, for the roots of these alien weeds are deeply embedded in the soil of Western civilization, where eradication is not a simple task. Ethnocentric pride, for example, remains as potent today as it was in former periods, and no human collectivity is ever immune to its siren voice. Colour consciousness, in spite of the determined struggle waged against this form of racial discrimination, has not disappeared, nor have the pejorative connotations associated with blackness (not to mention other "racial" colours). While modern black theologians have sought to overcome this negative dualism by endowing blackness with various positive meanings, including depth and mystery,[7] their efforts have not been entirely successful. Anti-blackness, as Joseph R. Washington has demonstrated recently in a lengthy survey of anti-black themes in English literature and religion, is extremely tenacious, and only a radical revision of the language and thought-forms of the Western mind could effect the desired change.[8] Myths, of course, can die, and I have suggested that the Aryan myth, at least in its nineteenth century form, has suffered this fate as a consequence of a general revulsion against the crimes of the German Third Reich. Racism, however, is not bound to a particular race myth, and continues to flourish in many parts of the contemporary world. Furthermore, the dualistic mentality, with its simplistic solutions to complex problems, notably the tendency to demonize one's enemies, is also very much alive, as the assorted terrorist fanatics of our day reveal. Their Manichaeism, whether expressed in political, social, or religious terms, is never far from a racial Manichaeism, and frequently moves in this direction.

At the same time, however, the current situation has special characteristics of its own. Not only has the Aryan account of white European (and American) origins been exposed as mythic rather than as historical or scientific, but even the term "race" has fallen from favour, along with the racial aspects of physical anthropology that once fascinated former generations. No one, therefore, apart from the adherents of neo-Nazi fringe groups such as the (American) "Church of the Aryan Nations,"[9] wishes to be identified as a racist, regardless of the nature of his or her views. Interestingly, contemporary neo-racist writers begin their books with the assertion that they are both anti-racist and anti-Nazi, and that their only goal is to enhance the future of humanity by exploring the biological aspects of human nature in light of the most recent developments in the life sciences.[10] Having stated their moral credentials, these new theoreticians of race invariably proceed to discredit the notion of human equality (and political egalitarianism) as a foolish illusion derived from abstract rationalistic assumptions rather than the findings of empirical science. Human beings, their readers are informed, are obviously *not* equal biologically; hence, a doctrinaire egalitarianism that insists on treating everyone in exactly the same way is a source of intellectual confusion as well as a public menace. If a society is to flourish, it must recognize innate human differences and design its social institutions accordingly. Not to do so is to ignore the "logic of the living,"[11] or the hereditarian factors that determine an important segment of our physical, psychological, mental, and even spiritual constitutions. Not everything that the Social Darwinists of the nineteenth century believed about the world was wrong, and not everything that the environmentalists of the twentieth century believe is right. Surely the time has come, it is argued, for the pendulum to swing in a reverse direction and for the neglected insights of men such as Francis Galton, the father of the intelligence controversy,[12] to receive their proper due. In this manner, the rudiments of a new scientific racism have reappeared in both Europe and North America among certain rightwing political interests, coalescing around the social use of IQ statistics and the doctrines of the sociobiologists.[13] It is no coincidence that some of the most visible signs of this revival have occurred in France, with its more than four million migrant workers, many of whom are North Africans.

A scientific neo-racism that dare not call itself by its proper name is not the sole manifestation of the racist spirit in western society today. Since the age in which racist ideology came to fruition was, by and large, an age of imperial power, racism and imperialism forged a mutual link that, if contemporary social criticism is correct, still endures.[14] Imperialism, like racism, is no longer in vogue, and the old colonial empires with their "patterns of dominance" have either vanished or been transformed into commonwealths of autonomous nations.[15] Nevertheless, racial domination persists, especially in the economic realm where the "Third World" exists in vassalage to the "First World" for the means of sustenance. Imperialism has only altered its form: "plus ça change, plus c'est la même chose." Since the terms Third and First World are social as well as geographical, such domination can occur within nations as well as between them, as when, for example, the system functions to exclude racial minorities (or even majorities) from "significant participation in its major social institutions."[16] While the process of exclusion can be overt, as in South Africa, it can also be covert, as in Canada, a country that does not consider itself to be contaminated by racism in the South African sense. Whether overt or covert, institutional racism is formidable and intractable, as well as "demonic" in its power.[17]

According to the social anthropologist Evelyn Kallen, racial elites construct "invisible walls" when they cannot build visible walls to prevent subject populations from stepping outside cultural, economic, political, and sometimes physical ghettos in so-called democratic communities.[18] Not only do these walls serve as social barriers, but they also keep the unwanted races in a state of lethargy and futility, the companions of political impotence and low self-esteem. In Canada, Kallen points out, inferior schools have been extremely effective in discouraging Indian and Inuit children from pursuing the dreams and ambitions that middle-class white children take for granted.[19] In the United States, the educational psychologist Arthur Jensen has argued that, as a consequence of genetic differences, certain racial groups, especially blacks, cannot be expected to succeed in conventional academic programmes, even if pre-school tuition is provided.[20] These children, therefore, must content themselves with lower status occupations in American society. By such subtle means, a racially-tainted pattern of dominance is perpetuated in the democratic West, vindicating, in Pierre Paraf's words, the tremendous "power and complexity of the racist phenomenon" of our time.[21]

This power and complexity are increased immeasurably if racism and imperialism are equated with capitalism and thus with the present economic and social scheme of things *per se*. Barbara Rogers has made this equation explicit;[22] so has Sheila Collins.[23] They argue that racism is more than ever at the core of the major policy decisions of the western industrial nations, especially, if the Canadian philosopher George Grant is correct, the Anglo-Saxon nations. According to Grant, Anglo-Saxon Protestants (i.e., British and American Calvinists), have been the "shock-troops" in the advance of capitalism and the prime bearers of its driving impulse to master nature, both human and non-human.[24] Not surprisingly, defenders of both capitalism and Anglo-Saxon Protestantism have reacted strongly against this accusation, for example, Ernest Lefever's castigation of Robert McAfee Brown for broadcasting America's international sins at the 1975 Assembly of the World Council of Churches (Nairobi).[25] Brown spoke Spanish, believing English to be the "language of imperialism." For Lefever, the World Council's financial support of potentially violent (and anti-white?) liberation movements on the African continent through its Programme to Combat Racism was a surrender to a "romanticized version" of the Third World that did not correspond to the real state of affairs.[26] To Brown, on the other hand, it was meaningless to oppose racism without opposing international capitalism as its ultimate institutionalized expression, and this meant opposing the United States.

With such charges and counter-charges, the entire issue has acquired a new dimension and cannot be resolved without resolving much larger questions. Can capitalism, i.e., the creation of wealth through the investment of capital, act only in an oppressive fashion? Is the capitalistic system really the problem, or are certain forms of capitalism, particularly monopolistic ones, and their abuse by blind or malevolent racial elites the true cause of exploitation in the underdeveloped countries? Even the famous eighteenth-century Scottish economist and moral philosopher Adam Smith, the father of laissez-faire theory and the darling of today's neo-conservatives, denounced the imperialistic side of economic expansionism as a costly and socially harmful enterprise because of the manner in which the "exclusive companies" tended to treat the "miserable and helpless" natives who fell under their sway.[27] His words are still relevant over two hundred years after the publication of his great treatise on the wealth of nations. While the capitalist/socialist debate cannot be settled in these pages, we can at least remind ourselves of its relevance to the problem of racism, especially in the context of Christian faith.

Certainly misery and helplessness, the fruits of exploitation, constitute important warning signs for those with eyes to see. *Ressentiment* sets class against class, nation against nation, and race against race. The world is full of unhealed wounds, and their persistent pain is bound to affect the shape of social attitudes in innumerable ways, some of them morbid. When feelings of disaffection and anger find an ideological matrix, the human community is divided against itself more deeply than ever. It is incumbent, then, on Christians who believe in social justice to struggle against the forces that inflict these wounds, and thus to ameliorate the causes of race hatred. But it is also incumbent on the same Christians not to succumb to racist temptations by turning to new racial nationalisms and racial Christs. "God is Red," declares the Indian theologian Vine Deloria,[28] with as much justification as any of the authors of the older assertions about the colour of God or the racial identity of Christ. Racism is eclectic in character, and easily accommodated to many diverse situations. Its myths are flexible and adaptable, and, if one myth perishes, another is always born or invented. The intellectual arsenal of pseudo-science is being replenished for the benefit of those who wish to cast their hostility in respectable or semi-respectable forms, especially those with political agendas.

Once the motivation exists, it is not difficult for the inventive mind to manufacture racist doctrines for public consumption without invoking the shibboleths of the past. Today, moreover, when refugees from every continent are seeking entry into the democratic nations of the West, and when the danger of a nativist backlash against their admission is a chronic problem, it is crucial for the churches to mount a constant vigil. "Sin's pathetic vicious circle," to quote Reinhold Niebuhr once again,[29] requires no less, and only grace can save us from its snares. One of these snares is the temptation to elevate ourselves by debasing others, and, as with every other temptation to which our sinful natures are prone, once we surrender to its charms, all manner of harm can follow. Wittingly or unwittingly, we can become the servants of evil, Christian and biblical morality notwithstanding, and Christianity can sink back into the twilight world of gods and idols before Christians are aware of the fact.

Notes

PREFACE

1 George L. Mosse, *Toward the Final Solution: A History of European Racism* (New York: Harper Colophon Books 1978), 128.
2 Marcus G. Singer, "Some Thoughts on Race and Racism," *Philosophia* 8, nos. 2–3 (November 1978): 153–83.
3 M. F. Ashley Montagu, *Man's Most Dangerous Myth: The Fallacy of Race* (Cleveland: World Publishing Co. 1964).
4 Ruth Benedict, *Race: Science and Politics* (New York: Viking Press 1947).
5 Singer, "Some Thoughts," 180.
6 George D. Kelsey, *Racism and the Christian Understanding of Man* (New York: Scribner's Sons 1965), 175.
7 *Rules of Discipline of the Religious Society of Friends* (1834).
8 John Wesley, "Thoughts on Slavery" (1774), republished in *The Works of the Reverend John Wesley*,[14] Vols. (London: J. Mason 1829–31) 11: 59–79.
9 Anatole Leroy-Beaulieu, *Israel among the Nations: A Study of the Jews and Antisemitism*, trans. Frances Hellman (New York: Putnam's Sons 1895), 98.

CHAPTER 1

1 The term was coined by Ludwig Gumplowitz in his *Rechtsstaat und Socialismus* (Innsbruck: Wagner 1881).
2 Cf. David R. Hughes and Evelyn Kallen, *The Anatomy of Racism: Canadian Dimensions* (Montreal: Harvest House 1974), 89.
3 J. N. Sevenster, *The Roots of Pagan Anti-semitism in the Ancient World* (Leiden: Brill 1975), ch. 1.

4 Aristotle *Politics* 1.6. Benjamin Jowett's translation.
5 Plato *Republic* 5.470.
6 Reinhold Niebuhr, *The Structure of Nations and Empires* (New York: Scribner's Sons 1959), 75.
7 Sevenster, *Roots of Pagan Anti-semitism*, passim. According to Hans Kohn (*The Idea of Nationalism: A Study in Its Origins and Background* [New York: Collier Books 1967], 51), the Greeks sometimes "expressed an unbridled and violent contempt surpassing the most chauvinistic utterances of modern nationalism." The Jews, of course, were also ethnocentric, but Jewish chosenness had a truly universalistic as well as a particularistic character because the God of Israel (Yahweh) was a god of universal justice who regarded *all* nations as his children: "'Are you not like the Ethiopians to me, / O people of Israel?' says the LORD. / 'Did I not bring up Israel from the land of Egypt, and the Philistines from Caphtor and the Syrians from Kir?'" (Amos 9:7).
8 Cf. John G. Gager, *The Origins of Anti-Semitism: Attitudes toward Judaism in Pagan and Christian Antiquity* (New York: Oxford University Press 1983), pt. 2.
9 Frank M. Snowden, Jr., *Blacks in Antiquity* (Cambridge, Mass.: Belknap Press, Harvard University Press 1970), 176.
10 Ibid., 144–6.
11 Ibid., 25.
12 Ibid., 189–90.
13 Ibid., 197.
14 Ibid., 199.
15 Marvin H. Pope, *Song of Songs: A New Translation with Introduction and Commentary*, The Anchor Bible (New York: Doubleday 1977), 310.
16 Origen, *Homiliae in Canticum Canticorum*, 1.6, cited in Snowden, *Blacks in Antiquity*, 199.
17 Maurice H. Farbridge, *Studies in Biblical and Semitic Symbolism* (London: Kegan Paul, Trench, Trübner 1923), 278.
18 Roger Bastide, "Color, Racism and Christianity," in John Hope Franklin, ed., *Color and Race* (Boston: Houghton, Mifflin 1968), 37.
19 Cf. Eulalio R. Baltzar, *The Dark Center: A Process Theology of Blackness* (New York: Paulist Press 1973), 1.
20 Snowden, *Blacks in Antiquity*, 205.
21 Ibid., 200. This description is based on Gregory of Nyssa.
22 Cf. Winthrop D. Jordan, *White over Black: American Attitudes toward the Negro: 1550–1812* (Baltimore: Penguin Books 1969), 18.
23 Probably during the late medieval and Renaissance periods when Christian writers became interested in Jewish books. See Jordan, *White over Black*, 18.

24 See *The Babylonian Talmud*, Sanhedrin 2, ed. I. Epstein, trans. H. Freedman (London: Soncino Press 1935), 745. In this instance, Ham is accused of having copulated in the ark.

25 Juan Comas, "Les Mythes raciaux," *Le Racisme devant la science* (UNESCO, Paris: Gallimard 1960), 14–15.

26 Cf. Thomas F. Gossett, *Race: The History of an Idea in America* (Dallas: Southern Methodist University Press 1963), 4.

27 Snowden, *Blacks in Antiquity*, 179.

28 Cf. Owen Chadwick, *Western Asceticism*, Library of Christian Classics (Philadelphia: Westminster Press 1958) 12: 61–2.

29 Baltazar, *Dark Center*, 11.

30 William R. Jones, *Is God a White Racist?: A Preamble to Black Theology* (Garden City, N.Y.: Doubleday 1973).

31 Bastide, "Colour, Racism and Christianity," 37.

32 Cf. Alan C. Kors and Edward Peters, *Witchcraft in Europe, 1100-1700: A Documentary History* (Philadelphia: University of Pennsylvania Press 1972), 40–2.

33 Norman Cohn, *The Pursuit of the Millennium* (New York: Oxford University Press 1970), 87.

34 Cf. John Block Friedman, *The Monstrous Races in Mediaeval Thought and Art* (Cambridge, Mass.: Harvard University Press 1981), 37.

35 Arend Th. van Leeuwen, *Christianity in World History*, trans. H. H. Hoskins (New York: Scribner's Sons 1964), 259. The thirteenth-century English "Mappa Mundi" (Hereford Cathedral) shows Jerusalem at the geographical centre of a word consisting of Europe, Asia, and Africa.

36 Ibid., 260.

37 Ibid., 264–5.

38 Jordan, *White over Black*, 38.

39 Ibid., 7.

40 Bastide, "Color, Racism and Christianity," 40–5.

41 "Apostolic Letter of Pope Paul III, A.D. 1537," cited in Thomas D'Arcy McGee, *The Catholic History of North America* (Boston: Patrick Donahoe 1855), 179–81.

42 Cf. Lewis Hanke, *Aristotle and the American Indians* (Bloomington: Indiana University Press 1959), 84. Unfortunately, however, Las Casas held less enlightened views regarding African blacks, whose importation as slaves he recommended for the Americas (cf. Colette Guillaumin, *L'Idéologie raciste: genèse et langage actuel* [Paris: Mouton 1972], 15).

43 Albert A. Sicroff, *Les Controverses des statuts de «pureté de sang" en Espagne du XVᵉ au XVIIᵉ siècle* (Paris: Didier 1960).

44 E.g., Rosemary Ruether, *Faith and Fratricide: The Theological Roots of Anti-Semitism* (New York: Seabury Press 1974), 203; Friedrich Heer,

God's First Love, trans. Geoffrey Skelton (New York: Weybright and Talley 1970), 115, 120–1.

45 Sicroff, *Les Controverses*, 36.

46 Ibid., 61.

47 Ibid., 36–53, especially Alonso de Cartegena's *Defensorium Unitatis Christianae* (1449).

48 Cf. Arthur O. Lovejoy, *The Great Chain of Being* (Cambridge, Mass.: Harvard University Press 1936), 65.

49 Jordan, *White over Black*, 223.

50 Ibid.

51 Aristotle, *Historia Animalium*, I: 8, 9, 10. See J. A. Smith and W. D. Ross, eds. and trans., *The Works of Aristotle*, vol. 4 (Oxford: Clarendon Press 1910).

52 John S. Haller, *Outcasts from Evolution: Scientific Attitudes of Racial Inferiority, 1859–1900* (Urbana: University of Illinois Press 1971), 9.

53 Peter Camper, *The Works of the Late Professor Camper, on the Connexion between the Science of Anatomy and the Arts of Drawing, Painting, Statuary...*, trans. T. Cogan (London: C. Dilly 1794), 50, cited in Jordan, *White over Black*, 225–6.

54 Anonymous tract cited in Thomas Vergil Peterson, *Ham and Japheth: The Mythic World of Whites in the Antebellum South* (Metuchen, N. J.: Scarecrow Press 1978), 147.

55 Ibid., 97–8.

56 Haller, *Outcasts from Evolution*, 74. According to Haller, Paracelsus, in 1520, first suggested that the different races were descended from different first parents.

57 Cf. Jordan, *White over Black*, ch. 12.

58 David Hume, "Of National Characters," *Essays* (London: Routledge and Sons 1906), 152–3, n1.

59 Richard H. Popkin, "The Philosophical Basis of Eighteenth-Century Racism," in Harold E. Pagliaro, ed., *Racism in the Eighteenth Century*, (Cleveland: Case Western University Press 1973), 246.

60 Baltazar, *Dark Center*, 29. See also Martin Barker's attack on Hume's philosophy of human nature (*The New Racism: Conservatives and the Ideology of the Tribe* [London: Junction Books 1981], 54–77).

61 Cf. Philip R. Sloan, "The Idea of Racial Degeneracy in Buffon's *Histoire Naturelle*," in Pagliaro, ed., *Racism*, 293–321.

62 Popkin, "Philosophical Basis," 247.

63 See ch. 4.

64 William Stanton, *The Leopard's Spots: Scientific Attitudes toward Race in America, 1815–59* (Chicago: University of Chicago Press 1960), 41. For another account of Morton and his associates, see Richard H. Popkin,

"Pre-Adamism in 19th Century American Thought: 'Speculative Biology' and Racism," *Philosophia* 8, nos. 2–3 (Nov. 1978): 205–39.

65   Stanton, *Leopard's Spots*, 41.

66   Ibid., 144.

67   Nancy Stepan, *The Idea of Race in Science: Great Britain, 1800–1960* (Hamden, Ct.: Archon Books 1982), 1.

68   Ruth Benedict, *Race: Science and Politics* (New York: Viking Press 1959), 111.

69   Cf. Michael D. Biddiss, *Father of Racist Ideology: The Social and Political Thought of Count Gobineau* (London: Weidenfeld and Nicolson 1970), 103. See also Marcus G. Singer, "Race and Racism," *Philosophia* 8, nos. 2–3 (Nov. 1978): 153–4.

70   The term "antisemitism" was probably coined by Wilhelm Marr. See Moshe Zimmermann, *Wilhelm Marr: The Patriarch of Antisemitism* (New York: Oxford University Press 1986), 112. Besides Marr, some of the proud antisemites were Eugen Dühring, Theodor Fritsch, Friedrich Lange, and Bernhard Förster (the brother-in-law of Friedrich Nietzsche).

71   Hannah Arendt, "Ideology and Terror: A Novel Form of Government," *The Origins of Totalitarianism* (New York: Meridian Books 1958), 469.

72   Kohn, *Idea*, 3; see also Elie Kedourie, *Nationalism* (New York: Praeger 1960), ch. 1.

73   Kedourie, *Nationalism*, 73–4.

74   According to Hannah Arendt, three great events stood at the threshold of the modern age and predetermined its character: "the discovery of America and the ensuing exploration of the whole earth; the Reformation, which ... started the twofold process of individual expropriation and the accumulation of social wealth; the invention of the telescope and the development of a new science that considers the nature of the earth from the viewpoint of the universe" (*The Human Condition* [New York: Doubleday 1969], 225).

75   Biddiss, *Father of Racist Ideology*, 104.

76   Théophile Simar, *Étude critique sur la formation de la doctrine des races au XVIIIᵉ siècle et son expansion au XIXᵉ siècle*, Académie Royale de Belgique, classes des lettres et des sciences morales et politiques, Mémoires, 2me sér., T. 16 (Bruxelles: Lamertin 1922), passim.

77   Ibid., 173,174, 187, 190. Simar disliked Nietzsche especially.

78   Paul Tillich, *Dynamics of Faith* (New York: Harper and Row 1957), ch. 1.

79   Paul Tillich, *Christianity and the Encounter of the World Religions* (New York: Columbia University Press 1963), ch. 1.

80   Jean-Paul Sartre, *Anti-Semite and Jew*, George J. Becker, trans. (New York: Schocken Books 1948), 10, 43. Manichaeism was a dualistic religion of antiquity with gnostic characteristics.

81   Ibid.

82 Northrop Frye, *The Great Code: The Bible and Literature* (Toronto: Academic Press Canada 1982), 33.
83 Paul Tillich, *The Socialist Decision*, trans. Franklin Sherman (New York: Harper and Row 1977), pt. 1.
84 Ibid., 41.
85 Mircea Eliade in reference to Jung (*Myths, Dreams and Mysteries*, trans. Philip Mairet [New York: Harper Torchbooks 1967], 25). Jung himself wrote as follows: "The revolution in our conscious outlook, brought about by the catastrophic results of the World War, shows itself in our inner life by the shattering of our faith in ourselves and our own worth ... How totally different did the world appear to mediaeval man! For him the earth was eternally fixed and at rest in the centre of the universe, encircled by the course of a sun that solicitously bestowed its warmth. Men were all children of God under the Most High, who prepared them for eternal blessedness; and all knew exactly what they should do and how they should conduct themselves in order to rise from a corruptible world to an incorruptible and joyous existence. Natural science has long ago torn this lovely veil to shreds. That age lies as far behind as childhood, when one's own father was unquestionably the handsomest and strongest man on earth." See Carl Jung, *Modern Man in Search of a Soul*, trans. W. S. Dell and Cary F. Baynes (New York: Harcourt, Brace and World 1933), 203–4.
86 Mircea Eliade, *Myth and Reality*, trans. Willard R. Trask (New York: Harper Torchbooks 1963), 183.
87 Ibid. Paul Ricœur writes in a similar vein of the existential significance of the archetypal "figure of the hero, the ancestor, the Titan, the first man, the demigod" in *The Symbolism of Evil*, trans. Emerson Buchanan (Boston: Beacon Press 1967), 162.
88 Arendt, *Origins of Totalitarianism*, 160, n6.
89 Christian Lassen (1800–1876) idealized the Aryans in his work on "Indian Antiquities" (*Indische Altertumskunde*, 1858–62) and Max Müller (1823–1900) followed suit. Both men were students of language and deeply interested in the racial origins of the Europeans. See George L. Mosse, *Toward the Final Solution: A History of European Racism* (New York: Harper Colophon Books 1978) 41–44.
90 Léon Poliakov, *The Aryan Myth: A History of Racist and Nationalist Ideas in Europe*, trans. Edmund Howard (London: Sussex University Press 1974), 191.

Not all contemporary historians regard the Aryan myth as false. The following modified version appears, for example, in a well-known and highly respected study in the history of religion.

"In the early history of Greece and Rome we met with bands of southward-surging Indo-Europeans; in northern Europe we find them everywhere ... One of the puzzles of history is where these people originated and what sent them on their far-flung journeys, radiating outward like the spokes of a wheel, south, west, north and southeast. But whatever moved them from their prehistoric homeland [in southern Russia and the Ukraine?] they succeeded ... not only in subjugating the resident tribes in their path, outnumbered though they were, but in superimposing their language upon those current among the tribes they conquered, together with many elements of their magic and religion. The ancient Celts and Teutons developed religious practices and beliefs which, in spite of assimilation of many variant local conceptions and customs, nevertheless illustrate what the original Indo-European world-view might be expected to become when not radically altered by the infusion of foreign ways of behaving and believing."

"Appearing in history later than the Celts, the Teutons, who were of somewhat purer Indo-European stock, began to press westward from the southern shores of the Baltic as Anglo-Saxons and Jutes, southward as Saxons, Alamanni, Lombards, Frisians, and Franks, northward as Scandinavians, and southeastward as Goths and Vandals." (David S. and John B. Noss, *Man's Religions*, 7th ed. [New York: Macmillan 1984], 61, 63.) The evidence cited in defence of this theory of European origins appears to be primarily linguistic and archaeological. Even allowing, however, for the elements of historicity in the myth – for example, the conquest of the Indus region by chariot-driving "Aryan" invaders during the second millennium BCE and the undoubted kinship between the "Indo-European" languages noted by the philologists – this account pretends to know too much. Poliakov (*Aryan Myth*, 209–10) notes that the British, who ruled India during the nineteenth century, did not like being told by Müller and others that they were the descendants of the ancestors of their own present-day subjects; consequently, the "prehistoric homeland" had to be moved westward. Furthermore, the picture of the ancient Aryans "radiating outward like the spokes of a wheel" reflects only the historians' imagination. How do the authors know that the Teutons were of "purer European stock" than the Celts? Consciously or unconsciously, they are simply echoing the racial and social views of men such as Robert Knox (chapter 4), who divided British society, largely for political reasons, into a superior Saxon and inferior Celtic race. It is interesting that Müller himself finally warned his contemporaries against the temptation to draw extravagant conclusions from linguistic arguments (Poliakov, *Aryan Myth*, 214). Apart from its racist motivations, the myth arose in large measure from the all-too-human tendency to simplify and magnify the fragmentary evidences of history.

91 Simar, *Étude critique*, 124; my translation.

92 Cited in *Gobineau: Selected Political Writings*, ed. Michael D. Biddiss (London: Cape 1970), 162–3.

93 Cf. Mosse, *Toward the Final Solution*, 2–3, 10–11.

94 So called by Biddiss in the title of his study of Gobineau.

95 Pierre L. van den Berghe, *Race and Racism: A Comparative Perspective* (New York: Wiley and Sons 1967), 15.

96 Haller, *Outcasts from Evolution*, esp. ch. 6.

97 Simar, *Étude critique*, 173–4.

98 Camille Spiess, *Impérialismes. La conception gobinienne de la race. Sa valeur au point de vue bio-psychologique* (Paris: Fiquière 1917).

99 Cf. Biddiss, *Selected Writings*, 178. Tocqueville warned Gobineau in a private letter of the danger of the latter's doctrines.

100 Pierre Paraf, *Le Racisme dans le monde* (Paris: Petite Bibliothèque Payot 1981), 69; my translation.

CHAPTER TWO

1 Cf. Norman Cohn, *The Pursuit of the Millennium* (New York: Oxford University Press 1970), 119-26.

2 Ibid., 125. The works referred to are Alfred Rosenberg, *Der Mythus des 20. Jahrhunderts* (München: Hoheneichen 1935); Jakob Wilhelm Hauer, *Deutsche Gotteschau* (Stuttgart: Gutbrod 1934); and Hans F. K. Günther, *Ritter, Tod und Teufel: Der heldische Gedanke* (München: J. F. Lehmann 1935).

3 Léon Poliakov, *The Aryan Myth: A History of Racist and Nationalist Ideas in Europe*, trans. Edmund Howard (London: Sussex University Press 1974), 78.

4 Cf. Paul Tillich, *A History of Christian Thought* (New York: Harper and Row 1968), 256; also Hans Kohn, *The Idea of Nationalism: A Study in Its Origins and Background* (New York: Collier Books 1967), 142.

5 Cf. Heiko A. Oberman, *The Roots of Anti-Semitism: In the Age of Renaissance and Reformation*, trans. James I. Porter (Philadelphia: Fortress Press 1981), pt. 3.

6 Kohn, *Idea of Nationalism*, 143.

7 Théophile Simar, *Étude critique sur la formation de la doctrine des races au XVIIIe siècle et son expansion au XIXe siècle*, Académie Royale de Belgique, classes des lettres et des sciences morales et politiques, Mémoires, 2me sér., T. 16 (Bruxelles: Lamertin 1922), 13.

8 For example, the great liberal Protestant theologians Adolf von Harnack and Wilhelm Herrmann who, along with ninety-one other German intellectuals, publicly supported the war aims of imperial Germany in 1914 on nationalistic grounds – the occasion, incidentally, of Karl Barth's famous *dies ater* (black day).

9 Otto Piper, *Recent Developments in German Protestantism* (London: SCM Press 1934), ch. 1.

10 Ibid.

11 Ibid., 10.

12 Ibid., 15.

13 Johann-Gottlieb Fichte, *Addresses to the German Nation*, trans. R. F. Jones and G. H. Turnbull, ed. George Armstrong Kelly (New York: Harper and Row 1968), 80–1.

14 Cf. Karl R. Popper, *The Open Society and Its Enemies*, 2 vols. (Princeton: Princeton University Press 1971), 2: 53.

15 Fichte, *Addresses*, 73–4.

16 Ibid.

17 Peter Viereck, *Metapolitics: The Roots of the Nazi Mind* (New York: Capricorn Books 1941), 60.

18 Fichte, *Addresses*, 184.

19 Simar, *Étude critique*, 106.

20 Fichte, *Addresses*, 184.

21 "Es bleibt auch bei diesem Evangelisten immer zweifelhaft, ob Jesus aus jüdischem Stamme sei, oder, falls er es doch etwa wäre, wie es mit seiner Abstammung sich eigentlich verhalte." (In this Evangelist it remains wholly doubtful whether or not Jesus was of Jewish origin at all, or, if he was, what his exact lineage was.) J. G. Fichte, *Werke*, ed. Fritz Medicus, 6 vols. (Leipzig: Verlag von Felix Meiner 1908–12), 4:105.

    For Fichte's view that only John contains a genuine understanding of the true meaning of religion and Christianity, see his *The Way towards the Blessed Life*, trans. William Smith (London: Chapman 1849), 95–6.

22 "Was it possible for him [John] to set forth more distinctly and forcibly the ground of this proposition: – that in God, and from God, there is nothing that arises or becomes; but that in him there is but an 'Is,' an Eternal Present; and that whatever has Existence must be originally with him, and must be himself? 'Away with that perplexing phantasm!' – might the Evangelist have added, had he wished to multiply words; 'away with that phantasm of a creation from God of something that is not in himself, and has not been eternally and necessarily in himself! – an emanation in which he is not himself present, but forsakes his work; an expulsion and separation from him that casts us out with desolate nothingness, and makes him our arbitrary and hostile Lord!'" (Ibid., 101–2.)

23 Fichte, *Werke*, 4: 105.

24 Cf. Koppel S. Pinson, *Pietism as a Factor in the Rise of German Nationalism* (New York: Columbia University Press 1934), 59.

25 Ibid.

26 Ibid., 49–50.

27 Ibid., 71.

28 Philip Jacob Spener, *Pia Desideria*, trans. Theodore G. Tappert (Philadelphia: Fortress Press 1952), 109–11.

29 Friedrich Schleiermacher, *On Religion: Speeches to Its Cultured Despisers*, trans. John Oman (New York: Harper and Brothers 1958), 9–11.

30 Cited in Pinson, *Pietism*, 98.

31 Friedrich Schleiermacher, "A Nation's Duty in a War for Freedom," *Selected Sermons of Schleiermacher*, trans. Mary F. Wilson (New York: Funk and Wagnalls n.d.), 73.

32 Pinson, *Pietism*, 202.

33 Schleiermacher, "A Nation's Duty," 73.

34 Cited in Pinson, *Pietism*, 148.

35 Friedrich Schleiermacher, "Necessity of the New Birth," *Selected Sermons*, 102.

36 Ibid., 90.

37 Albert Schweitzer, *The Quest of the Historical Jesus*, trans. W. Montgomery (London: Black 1948), 310.

38 Cf. Fritz Stern, *The Politics of Cultural Despair: A Study in the Rise of the Germanic Ideology* (Berkeley: University of California Press 1961), 41.

39 Paul de Lagarde, "Die Religion der Zukunft," *Deutsche Schriften*, 2 vols. (Munich: Lehmanns Verlag 1934), 1:262; my translation.

40 Stern, *Politics*, ch. 4.

41 Lagarde, "Die Religion der Zukunft," 285.

42 Stern, *Politics*, 61.

43 Cf. Viereck, *Metapolitics*, ch. 5. See also Jacob Katz, *From Prejudice to Destruction: Anti-Semitism, 1700–1933* (Cambridge, Mass.: Harvard University Press 1980), ch. 14.

44 Fritz Fischer, *War of Illusions: German Politics from 1911-1914*, trans. Marion Jackson (London: Chatto and Windus 1975), 29–30.

45 H. S. Chamberlain, *The Foundations of the Nineteenth Century*, trans. John Lees, 2 vols. (London: Bodley Head 1913), 1:211.

46 Ibid., 200.

47 Ibid., 224.

48 Ibid., 227.

49 Ibid., 237.

50 Ibid., 210.

51 Cf. Josephus, *Contra Apion*, bk. 1, 12.

52 Cf. Rosemary Ruether, *Faith and Fratricide: The Theological Roots of Anti-Semitism* (New York: Seabury Press 1974), ch. 3; James Parkes, *The Conflict of the Church and the Synagogue: A Study in the Origins of Antisemitism* (New York: Atheneum 1977), passim; Jules Isaac, *Jesus and Israel*, trans. Sally Gran (New York: Holt, Rinehart and Winston 1971), passim.

53 Especially ch. 23.
54 Roger Bastide, "Color, Racism and Christianity," in *Color and Race*, ed. John Hope Franklin (Boston: Houghton, Mifflin 1968), 37.
55 Otto Weininger, *Geschlecht und Charakter: eine prinzipielle Untersuchung* (Wienund Leipzig: W. Braummüller 1908).
56 Cf. George L. Mosse, *Germans and Jews: The Right, the Left, and the Search for a "Third Force" in Pre-Nazi Germany* (New York: Fertig 1970), 55.
57 This process of syncretism varied, however; Hauer, for example, dispensed with Christ (and every other mediator), asserting instead a mystical union between the indwelling God and the Human soul ("An Alien or a German Faith," in Wilhelm Hauer, Karl Heim, and Karl Adam, *Germany's New Religion*, trans. T. S. K. Scott-Craig and R. E. Davies [New York: Abingdon Press 1937], 49). Other apostles of a new Germanic religion, more attached to the figure of Jesus, identified him with the Teutonic sun god and the Virgin Mary with the "mother" of the Aryans! Cf. George L. Mosse, *The Crisis of German Ideology: Intellectual Origins of the Third Reich* (New York: Grosset and Dunlap 1964), 72.
58 Uriel Tal, *Christians and Jews in Germany: Religion, Politics and Ideology in the Second Reich, 1870–1914* (Ithaca: Cornell University Press 1975), 226.
59 Friedrich Nietzsche, *Twilight of the Idols, and the Anti-Christ*, trans. R. J. Hollingdale (Harmondsworth: Penguin Books 1968), 29.
60 Ibid., 141.
61 Cf. Walter Kaufmann, *Nietzsche: Philosopher, Psychologist, Antichrist* (Princeton: Princeton University Press 1974), 42.
62 "The Guiding Principles of the Faith Movement of the 'German Christians,' June 6, 1932," cited in Arthur C. Cochrane, *The Church's Confession under Hitler* (Philadelphia: Westminster Press 1962), 222–3.
63 Walter Grundmann, *Jesus der Galiläer und das Judentum* (Leipzig: Verlag George Wigand 1940).
64 E.g., Emanuel Hirsch, *Das kirchliche Wollen der Deutschen Christen* (Berlin: Verlag Max Grevemeyer 1933), 9–10; also D. Cajus Fabricus, *Positive Christianity in the Third Reich* (Dresden: Puschel 1937), ch. 6.
65 Cf. Fritz Stern, *Gold and Iron: Bismarck, Bleichröder and the Building of the German Empire* (New York: Knopf 1977), 512.
66 Ibid., 511.
67 Tal, *Christians and Jews*, ch. 2.
68 Ibid., 259.
69 Ibid., 257–8.
70 As expounded in his tract *Temporal Authority* (1523).
71 Tal, *Christians and Jews*, 100.

72 Ibid., 257.

73 Richard Gutteridge, *Open Thy Mouth for the Dumb!* (Oxford: Blackwell 1976), 9.

74 Wolfgang Tilgner, "Volk, Nation und Vaterland in protestantischen Denken zwischen Kaiserreich und Nationalsozialismus (ca. 1870–1933)," in Horst Zillessen, ed., *Volk, Nation, Vaterland.* (Gütersloh: Gütersloher Verlaghaus Gerd Mohn 1970), 138.

75 Ibid. (cited), 155; my translation.

76 Cited in Gunda Schneider-Flume, *Die politische Theologie Emanuel Hirschs, 1918–1933* (Bern: Herbert Lang 1971), 1; my translation.

77 Ibid., 2–3.

78 Ibid., 5–6.

79 Ibid., 8–9.

80 Søren Kierkegaard (Johannes de Silentio), *Fear and Trembling: A Dialectical Lyric*, trans. Robert Payne (London: Oxford University Press 1843), passim.

81 Schneider-Flume, *Die politische Theologie*, 10–11.

82 Cited in Schneider-Flume, *Die politische Theologie*, 160. Karl Barth's comment on Hirsch is apropos. "This basic theme [of Hirsch's Book *Die gegenwärtige geistige Lage im Spiegel philosophischer und theologischer Besinnung*] consists in the hypothesis that the present spiritual situation is to be 'interpreted' as a 'meeting with God.' Hirsch wants to build the Church on this rock and this rock only. It is from this viewpoint that he construes her preservation, her renovation, her task. His view of history is centered on this. The spirits are divided here for him. Here the worth, or lack of it, of all philosophy and theology is decided according to him. Within the framework of the recognition of this thesis he will speak of everything or a great deal; but, outside of this framework, of nothing at all. Into the reality affirmed in this thesis, theology and the church have to weave themselves, to let themselves be woven, to be woven together with it." (Karl Barth, *The German Church Conflict*, trans. P. T. A. Parker [London: Lutterworth Press 1965], 30.)

83 Karl Heim, *The Church of Christ and the Problems of the Day* (London: Scribner's Sons 1935), 33–4.

84 Helmut Thielicke, "Why the Holocaust?" *Christianity Today* 22, no. 8 (27 January 1978): 516.

85 Fritz K. Ringer, "The Perversion of Ideas in Weimar Universities," in Henry Friedlander and Sybil Milton, eds., *The Holocaust: Ideology, Bureaucracy and Genocide* (Millwood, N.Y.: Kraus International 1981), 57.

86 Ernst C. Helmreich, *The German Churches under Hitler: Background, Struggle and Epilogue* (Detroit: Wayne State University Press 1979), 128.

87   Martin Luther, *Temporal Authority: To What Extent Should It Be Obeyed?*,
      trans. J. J. Schindel, *Luther's Works*, ed. Walther I. Brandt, (Philadelphia:
      Muhlenberg Press 1962), 113. Civil war, of course, generally produces
      arguments in favour of strong government. Like Luther, Thomas Hobbes
      reacted in this fashion to the social and political turmoil of his day
      (Cromwellian England) in his work *Leviathan*.

88   Gutteridge, *Open Thy Mouth*, 45.

89   Ibid.

90   Paul Althaus, *Christus und die deutsche Seele* (Gütersloh: Bertelsmann
      1934), 34; my translation.

91   To Hauer, while God was eternal, everything else was trapped in the
      cycle of endless change. "Forms of religion and brands of faith come
      into being and pass away, but the ground out of which they arise
      remains; the power to experience the divine and to give it form continues
      operating without cessation in man" (cited in Arthur Frey, *Cross and
      Swastika*, trans. J. Strathearn McNab [London: SCM Press 1938], 91).
      The gods are not God; hence they perish like mortals, including the
      new gods of modern religion, which, in Hauer's extreme tribalistic
      nationalism included even the racial deities of blood, *Volk*, and soil.
      Only their impersonal ground, ultimately indistinguishable from nature
      and its invisible depths, remains the same. Because, according to God's
      "Eternal Will," the sun, having appeared between the clouds, must
      disappear again behind their dark masses, because living things, having
      been born, must die, death with its "silent hand-clasp" becomes life's
      "supreme moment," not only its physical termination but its *raison
      d'être*, its heroic consummation and spiritual completion. (Hauer, "An
      Alien or a German Faith?," 63.) Death, in other words, is the point
      of life, to be celebrated as much as birth since it signifies our return
      to the primal ground of our being, the embrace of God. Yet birth is
      to be celebrated as well: the sun must rise before it can set, and youth
      must taste the "wine's dark strength" – the pulsing blood of nation
      and race – before it drinks the still darker cup of death. (Frey, *Cross
      and Swastika*, 97.) Should not the reborn Germany rejoice in its racial
      youth before it bows before its eventual extinction? Thus Hauer made
      everything, even Germany, sink back into nature and its cosmic rhythms.

92   Tilgner, "Volk, Nation und Vaterland," in Zillessen, ed., *Volk, Nation,
      Vaterland*, 162.

93   Emil Brunner, *The Divine Imperative*, trans. Olive Wyon (Philadelphia:
      Westminster Press 1947), 456.

94   Ibid., 458.

95   Friedrich Gogarten, *Politische Ethik* (Jena: Eugen Diederichs Verlag 1932),
      58; my translation.

96   Larry Shiner, *The Secularization of History: An Introduction to the Theology of Friedrich Gogarten* (Nashville, Tenn.: Abingdon Press 1966), 205.

97   Ibid., 208. Gogarten, however, was never personally a National Socialist and soon dissociated himself from the German Christians.

98   Martin Buber, *Between Man and Man*, trans. Ronald Gregor Smith (London: Collins 1961), 100–4.

99   Shiner, *Secularization of History*, 211.

100   Friedrich Gogarten, *Religion und Volkstum* (Jena: Eugen Diederichs Verlag 1915), 13; my translation.

101   Shiner, *Secularization of History*, 211.

102   Cited in James A. Zabel, *Nazism and the Pastors* (Missoula, Mon.: Scholars Press 1976), 66.

103   Ibid., 66–7.

104   Cited in Gutteridge, *Open Thy Mouth*, 44.

105   Ibid.

106   Brunner, *The Divine Imperative*, 698. For a detailed examination of Althaus' theological and political views, see Robert P. Erickson, *Theologians under Hitler: Gerhard Kittel, Paul Althaus and Emanuel Hirsch* (New Haven: Yale University Press 1985), ch. 3.

107   Paul Althaus, *Die deutsche Stunde der Kirche* (Göttingen: n.p. 1934).

108   Zabel,*Nazism and the Pastors*, 67.

109   Cf. Nils Ehrenstrom, *Christian Faith and the Modern State*, trans. Denzil Patrick and Olive Wyon (London: SCM Press 1937), 122.

110   Ibid. (cited), 124.

111   Brunner discusses this (*Divine Imperative*, 697) with particular reference to Heinrich von Treitschke's *Deutsche Geschichte im neunzehnten Jahrhundert* (1886–99). In these lectures, war was glorified as the "school" of morality and idealism in which the nations recovered a sense of energy and the spirit of sacrifice.

112   Winthrop D. Jordan, *White over Black: American Attitudes toward the Negro: 1550–1812* (Baltimore: Penguin Books 1969), 165–6.

113   Chamberlain, *Foundations*, 1: 519–21.

114   Hirsch, *Das kirchliche Wollen*, 11; my translation.

115   Mosse, *Germans and Jews*, 85.

116   Cf. Ronald Stone, *Paul Tillich's Radical Social Thought* (Atlanta: John Knox Press 1980), esp. ch. 5.

117   Cf. Wilhelm and Marion Pauck, *Paul Tillich: His Life and Thought*, 2 vols. (New York: Harper and Row 1976), 1: 153. The Paucks describe Hirsch in fairly sympathetic terms. See also A. James Reimer, "Theological Method and Political Ethics: The Paul Tillich-Emanuel Hirsch Debate," *Journal of the American Academy of Religion* 47, no. 1 (March 1979): 171–92.

118   Tilgner, "Volk, Nation und Vaterland," in Zillessen, ed., *Volk, Nation, Vaterland*, 166.

119 Emanuel Hirsch, *Ethos und Evangelium* (Berlin: de Gruyter 1966), 264. For recent evaluations of Hirsch, see A. James Reimer, "The Theology of Barmen: Its Partisan-Political Dimension," *Toronto Journal of Theology* 1, no. 2 (Fall 1985): 155–74, and Erickson, *Theologians under Hitler*, ch. 4.

120 Cited in Gutteridge, *Open Thy Mouth*, 94.

121 "Theologisches Gutachten über die Zulassung von Christen judischer herkunft zu den Amtern der Deutschen Evangelischen Kirche," in Kurt Dietrich Schmidt, ed., *Die Bekenntnisse und grundsätzlichen Ausserungen zur Kirchenfrage des Jahres 1933* (Göttingen: Vandenhoeck und Reprecht 1937), 184.

122 Ibid.

123 Ibid., 185.

124 Gutteridge, *Open Thy Mouth*, 109–10.

125 Helmreich, *The German Churches under Hitler*; John S. Conway, *The Nazi Persecution of the Churches, 1933–45* (London: Weidenfeld and Nicolson 1968); Klaus Scholder, *Die Kirchen und das Dritte Reich* (Berlin: Ullstein 1977).

126 Dietrich Bonhoeffer, *No Rusty Swords*, trans. John Bowden (London: Collins 1965): 217–25.

127 Piper, *Recent Developments in German Protestantism*, 150.

128 Karl Holl, *The Cultural Significance of the Reformation*, trans. Karl and Barbara Herta and John H. Lichtblau (New York: Meridian Books 1959), 63.

CHAPTER THREE

1 Théophile Simar, *Étude critique sur la formation de la doctrine des races au XVIIIᵉ siècle et son expansion au XIXᵉ siècle*, Académie Royale de Belgique, classes des lettres et des sciences morales et politiques, Mémoires, 2me sér., T. 16 (Bruxelles: Lamertin 1922), 19; my translation.

2 Francis Hotman, *Franco-Gallia* (1573), ch. 10. Cited in Julian H. Franklin, ed., *Constitutionalism and Resistance in the Sixteenth Century*, (New York: Pegasus 1969), 65.

3 Count Henri de Boulainvilliers, *Histoire de l'ancient gouvernement de la France* (1727). For a convenient summary of Boulainvilliers' view, see Jacques Barzun, *The French Race* (Port Washington, N.Y.: Kennikat Press 1966), 138–47.

4 Alexis de Tocqueville, *L'Ancien Régime et la révolution* (Paris: Lévy Frères 1860), 152.

5 Emmanuel Joseph Sieyès, *Qu'est-ce le tiers-état?* (1789). Cited in Barzun, *The French Race*, 248.

6 Michael D. Biddiss, *Father of Racist Ideology: The Social and Political Thought of Count Gobineau* (London: Weidenfeld and Nicolson 1970), 105.

7   Ibid., 109.

8   William Blake, "And Did Those Feet in Ancient Time" in *William Blake: The Complete Poems*, ed. Alicia Ostriker (Harmondsworth: Penguin Books 1977), 514.

9   Dirk J. Struik, "Introduction" to Karl Marx's *Economic and Philosophic Manuscripts of 1844*, trans. Martin Milligan (New York: International Publishers 1964), 50.

10 For example, Paul de Lagarde in Germany (although Lagarde can be classified as a revolutionary as well as a reactionary). Cf. Fritz Stern, *The Politics of Cultural Despair: A Study in the Rise of the Germanic Ideology* (Berkeley: University of California Press 1961), 60–1.

11 Mircea Eliade, *Myth and Reality*, trans. Willard R. Trask (New York: Harper Torchbooks 1963), 183.

12 Biddiss, *Father of Racist Ideology*, 112.

13 Edmund Burke, "Letter on a Regicide Peace" in *The Writings and Speeches of Edmund Burke* 5 vols. (Toronto: Morang 1901) 5: 237.

14 Edmund Burke, *Reflections on the Revolution in France* (Harmondsworth: Penguin Books 1969), 301.

15 Cf. Ernest R. Sandeen, *The Roots of Fundamentalism* (Chicago: University of Chicago Press 1970), 5–6.

16 Biddiss, *Father of Racist Ideology*, 97.

17 Cf. *Gobineau's Selected Political Writings*, ed. Michael D. Biddiss (London: Cape 1970), 96.

18 Max Scheler, *Ressentiment*, trans. William W. Holdheim (New York: Shocken Books 1972).

19 Ibid., 67. Scheler cites Nietzsche (*Genealogy of Morals*, pt. 1, 15) who, in turn, cites Tertullian (*De spectaculis*, ch. 29–30). Tertullian had good reason to be disgusted at the cruelties of the games of the ancient amphitheatre. Nietzsche's (and Scheler's) indictment is not altogether fair.

20 George L. Mosse, *Toward the Final Solution: A History of European Racism* (New York: Harper Colophon Books 1978), 53.

21 Biddiss, *Father of Racist Ideology*, 124.

22 Léon Poliakov, *The Aryan Myth: A History of Racist and Nationalist Ideas in Europe*, trans. Edmund Howard (London: Sussex University Press 1974), 272–3.

23 Ibid.

24 Biddiss, *Father of Racist Ideology*, 251.

25 Jacob Katz, *From Prejudice to Destruction: Anti-Semitism, 1700–1933* (Cambridge, Mass.: Harvard University Press 1980), 136.

26 Ernest Renan, *Essai psychologique sur Jésus-Christ* (Paris: La Connaissance 1921), 55–7.

27 Ernest Renan, *The Life of Jesus* (London: Watts 1935), 37.

28 Ibid., 225.
29 Michael R. Marrus, *The Politics of Assimilation* (Oxford: Clarendon Press 1971), 11–12.
30 Fadiey Lovsky, *Antisémitisme et mystère d'Israel* (Paris: Edition Albin Michel 1955), 278.
31 Ernst Nolte, *Three Faces of Fascism: Action Française, Italian Fascism, National Socialism*, trans. Leila Vennewitz (New York: Mentor Books 1969), 69.
32 In 1845.
33 Louis Jacolliot, *Bible dans l'Inde: Vie de Iezeus Christna* (Paris: A. Lacroix 1869); cf. Poliakov, *The Aryan Myth*, 209.
34 Gustave Tridon, *Du Molochisme Juif* (Bruxelles: E. Maheu 1884); Albert Regnard, *Aryens et Sémites: le bilan du judaïsme et du christianisme* (Paris: E. Denta 1890). Cf. Edmund Silberner, "French Socialism and the Jewish Question, 1865-1914," *Historia Judaica* 16, pt. 1 (April 1954): 6–7. Tridon died in 1871, leaving his tract to be published posthumously.
35 Silberner, "French Socialism," 6–7.
36 Cf. Edmund Silberner, *The Anti-Semitic Tradition in Modern Socialism*, Inaugural Address Delivered at the Hebrew University on 4 January, 1953, Jerusalem, 11.
37 Edmond Picard, *L'Aryano-Sémitisme* (Bruxelles: P. Lacomblez 1899).
38 Karl Marx, *Zur Judenfrage*, republished in *Karl Marx on Religion*, ed. by Saul K. Padoue (New York: McGraw-Hill 1974), 169–192, (1844).
39 Edmund Silberner, "Two Studies in Modern Anti-Semitism," *Historia Judaica* 14, pt. 2 (October 1952): 113.
40 Paul Broca, *Mémoires d'anthropologie* (Paris: Reinwald 1879).
41 Armand de Quatrefages, *La Race prussienne* (Pans: Hachette 1871).
42 Georges Vacher de Lapouge, *L'Aryan: son rôle social* (Paris: A. Fontemoing 1899).
43 Michael Hammond, "Anthropology as a Weapon of Social Combat in Late Nineteenth-Century France," *Journal of the History of the Behavioral Sciences* 16 (1980): 126.
44 Jean-Paul Sartre, *Anti-Semite and Jew*, trans. George J. Becker (New York: Schocken Books 1948), 45.
45 Edouard Drumont, *La France juive*, tome premier, nouv. éd. (Paris: C. Marpon et E. Flammarion 1885), 9; my translation.
46 Robert F. Brynes, *Antisemitism in Modern France* (New Brunswick: Rutgers University Press 1950), 1: 163.
47 Adolf Hitler, *Mein Kampf*, trans. Ralph Manheim (Boston: Houghton Mifflin 1943), 65: "If ... the Jew is victorious over the other peoples of the world, his crown will be the funeral wreath of humanity and this planet will, as it did thousands of years ago, move through the

ether devoid of men. Eternal Nature inexorably avenges the infringement of her commands."

48 Cf. Norman Cohn, *Warrant for Genocide: The Myth of the Jewish World Conspiracy and the Protocols of the Elders of Zion* (Harmondsworth: Penguin Books 1967), 31, n2.

49 Ibid., 29–30.

50 Jacob Katz, *Jews and Freemasons in Europe, 1723-1939*, trans. Leonard Oschry (Cambridge, Mass.: Harvard University Press 1970), 131.

51 Henri Gougenot des Mousseaux, *Le Juif, le judaisme et la judaisation des peuples chrétiens* (Paris: Wattelier 1869).

52 Ernest Jouin, *La Judéo-Maçonnerie et l'Église Catholique* (Paris: Émile-Paul Frères 1921), 116.

53 Lovsky, *Antisémitisme*, ch. 9.

54 For example, Louis de Bonald: ibid., 317.

55 This passage from Leo XIII's encyclical dealing with secret societies (April 1884) is cited by Richard Henry Clarke, *The Life of His Holiness ... Together with Extracts from His Pastorals and Encyclicals* (Philadelphia: Ziegler 1903), 354.

56 Lovsky, *Antisémitisme*, 26.

57 Cf. Pierre Sorlin, *"La Croix" et les Juifs (1880-1899): contribution à l'histoire de l'antisémitisme contemporain* (Paris: Grasset 1967), 162.

58 Pierre Pierrard, *Juifs et catholiques français: de Drumont à Jules Isaac (1886-1945)* (Paris: Rayard 1970), 73, 115. Even before Dreyfus became a *cause célèbre*, Desportes "manifesta un antisémitisme féroce" and Delassus detected behind every modernist, Freemason and democrat "l'ombre grotesque du juif au nez crochu."

59 Jouin, *La Judéo-Maçonnerie*, 116–17. Converted Jews retain a Jewish temperament and therefore cannot accept "les dons de lumière et de grâce que pour réaliser leur idéal de domination universelle."

60 Henri de Lubac, "Un Nouveau 'Front' Religieux," *Israel et la foi chrétienne* (Fribourg: Librairie de l'Université 1942), 36–7.

61 Cf. Michael R. Marrus and Robert O. Paxton, *Vichy France and the Jews* (New York: Basic Books 1981), esp. 270–9.

62 Stephen Wilson, *Ideology and Experience: Antisemitism in France at the Time of the Dreyfus Affair* (Teaneck, N.J.: Fairleigh Dickinson University Press 1982), esp. chs. 14 and 16.

63 Nolte, *Three Faces of Fascism*, 111.

64 Pius XI later (1937) denounced racism in Germany in his powerful encylical *Mit brennender Sorge*.

65 Cf. Oscar L. Amal, *Ambivalent Alliance: The Catholic Church and The Action Française 1899–1939* (Pittsburgh: University of Pittsburgh Press 1985), 19.

66 Cited in William C. Buthman, *The Rise of Integral Nationalism in France: With Special Reference to the Ideas and Activities of Charles Maurras* (New York: Octagon Books 1970), 221.
67 Ibid. (cited), 152.
68 Ibid. (cited).
69 Cf. Robert Soucy, *Fascism in France: The Case of Maurice Barrès* (Berkeley: University of California Press 1972), 137.
70 Ibid. (cited), 143.
71 Ibid., 114.

CHAPTER FOUR

1 E.g., Gerrard Winstanley. In his study *Puritanism and Revolution: Studies in Interpretation of the English Revolution of the 17ᵗʰ Century* (London: Secker and Warburg 1958), Christopher Hill argues that the myth actually had medieval origins, but was rediscovered by anti-royalist sectarians such as Winstanley during the seventeenth century.
2 Gerrard Winstanley, *The True Levellers' Standard Advanced* (1649), cited in *Winstanley: The Law of Freedom and Other Writings*, ed. Christopher Hill (Harmondsworth: Penguin Books 1973), 86.
3 Léon Poliakov, *The Aryan Myth: A History of Racist and Nationalist Ideas in Europe*, trans. Edmund Howard (London: Sussex University Press 1974), 49.
4 Ibid., 49–50.
5 Michael P. Banton, *The Idea of Race* (London: Tavistock Publications 1977), ch. 4.
6 Hannah Arendt, *The Origins of Totalitarianism* (New York: Meridian Books 1948), 175–6.
7 *Tancred* (1847), new ed. (London: Longmans, Green 1894). According to Léon Poliakov (*Le Racisme* [Paris: Editions Seghers 1976], 73), Gobineau may actually have been inspired by Disraeli's dictum.
8 Cf. George L. Mosse, *Toward the Final Solution: A History of European Racism* (New York: Harper Colophon Books 1978), 67.
9 Robert Knox, *The Races of Men* (London: Renshaw 1862; 2nd ed. of *Types of Men*, 1850), 11.
10 Cf. Mosse, *Toward the Final Solution*, 68–9.
11 Knox, *Races of Men*, 5.
12 Ibid., 11.
13 Ibid.
14 Ibid., 30.
15 Ibid., 37. Knox borrowed this concept from Geoffrey St. Hilaire in Paris (see Nancy Stepan, *The Idea of Race in Science: Great Britain, 1800–1960* [Hamden, Ct.: Archon Books 1982], 42).

16 Ibid., 30.
17 Ibid., 38.
18 Poliakov, *The Aryan Myth*, 232.
19 Loren R. Graham, *Between Science and Values* (New York: Columbia University Press 1981), passim.
20 Charles Darwin, *The Descent of Man* (Boston: Caldwell 1874), 612.
21 Ibid., 174.
22 Charles Wentworth Dilke, *Greater Britain* (Philadelphia: Lippincott 1869), 347.
23 Ibid.
24 Ibid., 348.
25 Thomas F. Gossett, *Race: The History of an Idea in America* (Dallas: Southern Methodist University Press 1963), 111–12.
26 Ibid., 126–7.
27 Herbert Spencer, "Mr. Martineau on Evolution," *Essays: Scientific, Political and Speculative*, 3 vols. (New York: Appleton 1896), 1: 379.
28 Herbert Spencer, "Militancy and Industrialism," rpt. in *Herbert Spencer on Social Evolution: Selected Writings*, ed. J. D. Y. Peel (Chicago: University of Chicago Press 1972), 149–50.
29 Herbert Spencer, "The Americans," *Essays*, 3: 480.
30 J. D. Y. Peel, *Herbert Spencer: The Evolution of a Sociologist* (New York: Basic Books 1971), 144–5.
31 Cf. Richard Hofstadter, *Social Darwinism in American Thought* (New York: George Braziller 1944), 41.
32 John S. Haller, *Outcasts from Evolution: Scientific Attitudes of Racial Inferiority, 1859–1900* (Urbana: University of Illinois Press 1971), 121–32, esp. 127.
33 Ibid., ix.
34 John Fiske, *American Political Ideas* (New York: Harper 1844), 28.
35 Ibid., 56.
36 Ibid., 129.
37 Ibid., 143.
38 Ibid., 141.
39 Hofstadter, *Social Darwinism in American Thought*, 184.
40 Thomas Carlyle, *Occasional Discourse on the Nigger Question*, (1853) republished in Carlyle's *Latter-Day Pamphlets*, M. K. Goldberg and J. P. Seigel, eds. (Canadian Federation for the Humanities 1983), 427.
41 H. Shelton Smith, *In His Image, But ...: Racism in Southern Religion, 1780–1910* (Durham, N.C.: Duke University Press 1972), 262.
42 Jean Russell, *God's Lost Cause: A Study of the Church and the Racial Problem* (London: SCM Press 1968), 79.
43 Walter Rauschenbusch, *Christianizing the Social Order* (New York: Macmillan 1912).

44 Josiah Strong, *Our Country: Its Possible Future and Its Present Crisis* (New York: Baker and Taylor 1885), 160.
45 Ibid., 166.
46 Ibid., 168.
47 Ibid., 174.
48 Josiah Strong, *The New Era; or, The Coming Kingdom* (New York: Baker and Taylor 1893), 69-70.
49 Ibid.
50 Ibid., 71.
51 Strong, *Our Country*, 176–8.
52 Ibid., 160.
53 Strong, *New Era*, ch. 5.
54 Ibid., 94.
55 Ibid., 104–5.
56 See ch. 5 following.
57 Ibid., 354.
58 Ibid., 81.
59 Gossett, *Race*, ch. 8.
60 Walter Rauschenbusch, *Christianizing the Social Order* (New York: Macmillan 1913), 375.
61 Walter Rauschenbusch, *Christianity and the Social Crisis* (New York: Macmillan 1911), 222.
62 Rauschenbusch, *Christianizing the Social Order*, 154.
63 Walter Rauschenbusch, "The Ideals of Social Reformers," cited in *The Social Gospel in America*, ed. Robert T. Handy (New York: Oxford University Press 1966), 287.
64 Smith, *In His Image*, 262–3.
65 Ibid., ch. 6.
66 Ibid., 274-7.
67 J. S. Woodsworth, *Strangers within Our Gates* (1909; rpt. Toronto: University of Toronto Press 1972), 181.
68 S. D. Chown, "How Shall the Foreigners Govern Us?" *Christian Guardian*, 81, no. 8 (23 February 1910): 8.
69 Madison Grant, *The Passing of the Great Race* (New York: Scribner's Sons 1923), 89.
70 Ibid., 263.
71 Ibid., 67.
72 Ibid., 167.
73 Ibid., 230.
74 Ford's newspaper, the *Dearborn Independent*, the vehicle of his antisemitic ideas, had a circulation of about 300,000. For a good account, see Norman Cohn, *Warrant for Genocide: The Myth of the Jewish World Conspiracy*

and the Protocols of the Elders of Zion (Harmondsworth: Penguin Books 1967), ch. 7.

75 The older New England patrician Henry Adams (1838–1918), the descendant of two American presidents, also reacted to the decline of Anglo-Saxon dominance in a changing America (and his own failing personal fortunes) by turning to racism and antisemitism: another clear case of *ressentiment*. For a good account of Adams, see E. Digby Baltzell, *The Protestant Establishment: Aristocracy and Caste in America* (London: Secker and Warburg 1964), 90–3. Grant's contemporary, T. Lothrop Stoddard, published *The Rising Tide of Color against White World-Supremacy* (New York: Scribner's 1920) and *The Revolt against Civilization: The Menace of the Underman* (New York: Chapman and Hall 1923) during the same era. It is worth noting, as a matter of record, that both Grant and Stoddard were castigated on Christian grounds by J. H. Oldham, the author of the still relevant and prophetic *Christianity and the Race Problem* (London: SCM 1924).

76 Ernst Nolte, *Three Faces of Fascism: Action Française, Italian Fascism, National Socialism*, trans. Leila Vennewitz (New York: Mentor Books 1969), 141.

77 Grant, *Passing of the Great Race*, xxxiii. Cf. Moshe Zimmermann, *Wilhelm Marr: The Patriarch of Antisemitism* (New York: Oxford University Press 1986).

78 John Enoch Powell, *Still to Decide*, ed. John Wood (London: Batford 1972), 201. Long before Powell, such nativist groups as the "Britons" and the "Imperial Fascist League" blamed aliens (in this case, Jews) for the decline of Britain and the British way of life, while calling for their expulsion. Like the French racists, moreover, their leaders contrasted an ideal past with a corrupt present – the beautiful England that used to be and is no more with the decadent England of their day – and painted the contrast in racist terms. Even during the 1920s it was not unusual for rightwing politicians and ideologues to lament the loss of British power in the world by indulging in extreme nationalism, racism and antisemitism. For a good account, see Gisela C. Lebzelter, *Political Anti-Semitism in England, 1918–1939* (New York: Holmes and Meier 1978).

79 Powell, *Still to Decide*, 164.

80 John Enoch Powell, *Freedom and Reality*, ed. John Wood (Kingswood, Surrey: Elliot Right Way Books 1969), 313. On the question of Powell's racism, see his revealing 1978 off-the-cuff interview with the German magazine *Der Spiegel*, translated and published in the *New Statesman*, 13 October 1978, 460–1.

81 Powell was defeated in his Northern Irish Constituency in the 1987 British general election.

CHAPTER FIVE

1   From Robert Bellah, "Civil Religion in America," *Daedalus* (Winter 1967): 1–21, and other writings.

2   It is likely, however, that a strain of Aryan science entered the Afrikaner nationalist mind through Afrikaner intellectuals who studied at German universities during the Third Reich, although, according to Dr. Beyers Naudé (in a private conversation with the author), the true extent of this influence cannot be determined until the secret papers of the Broederbond are examined. Piet Meyer, for example, was attracted to Nazi racial ideas: Meyer was an important figure in the Afrikaner trade-union movement as well as the South African Broadcasting Corporation. He was also head of the Broederbond. Another young Afrikaner influenced by German racial ideology was J. Albert Coetzee. See Leonard Thompson, *The Political Mythology of Apartheid* (New Haven: Yale University Press 1985), 42–3.

3   W. A. de Klerk, *The Puritans in Africa: A Story of Afrikanerdom* (London: Collings 1975).

4   Cf. T. Dunbar Moodie, *The Rise of Afrikanerdom: Power, Apartheid, and the Afrikaner Civil Religion* (Berkeley: University of California Press 1975), chs. 1 and 2. This mythology, however, arose largely *after* the historic events which the Afrikaner myth-makers enshrined in their sacred histories of the nation; consequently, a great deal of falsification was employed. Compare, for example, the difference between what actually happened at Blood River and the later mythological version of the "covenant" in Afrikaner nationalism (Thompson, *Political Mythology*, 144–88).

5   Moodie, *Rise of Afrikanerdom*, 13–14.

6   Irving Hexham, *The Irony of Apartheid: The Struggle for National Independence of Afrikaner Civil Religion against British Imperialism* (New York: Mellen Press 1981), 33–46.

7   Ibid. (cited), 40.

8   Ibid., 41.

9   Ibid.

10   Moodie, *Rise of Afrikanerdom*, 15.

11   Ibid.

12   Ibid.

13   Hexham, *Irony of Apartheid*, 40.

14   Théophile Simar, *Étude critique sur la formation de la doctrine des races au XVIIIᵉ siècle et son expansion au XIXᵉ siècle*, Académie Royale de Belgique, classes des lettres et des sciences morales et politiques, Mémoires, 2me sér., T. 16 (Bruxelles: Lamertin 1922), 58.

15   Moodie, *Rise of Afrikanerdom*, 61.

16 So John W. de Gruchy remarks in *Bonhoeffer and South Africa: Theology in Dialogue* (Grand Rapids, Mich.: Eerdmans 1984), 107.

17 Abraham Kuyper, *Calvinism: The L. P. Stone Lectures for 1898–1899* (New York: Revell 1899), lect. 3. Kuyper's only apparent connection with South Africa, apart from the Afrikaner students influenced by his ideas, was his strongly anti-British posture during the Anglo-Boer War (Ibid., 45).

18 Ibid., 99.

19 Ibid., 1.

20 Ibid., 37.

21 De Gruchy, *Bonhoeffer and South Africa*, 110; Moodie, *Rise of Afrikanerdom*, 56, n5.

22 Kuyper, *Calvinism*, 115.

23 Ibid., 116.

24 Ibid., 119.

25 Herman Dooyeweerd, *Roots of Western Culture: Pagan, Secular, and Christian Options*, trans. John Kraay, ed. Mark Vander Vennen and Bernard Zylstra (Toronto: Wedge Publishing Foundation 1979), 181–2. Kuyper himself wrote as follows (*Calvinism*, 103): "For God created the nations. They exist for Him. They are His own. And therefore all these nations, and in them all humanity, must exist for His glory and consequently after His ordinances, in order that in their well-being, when they walk after His ordinances, His divine wisdom may shine forth."

26 Dooyeweerd, *Roots of Western Culture*, 51.

27 Herbert Marcuse, *Reason and Revolution: Hegel and the Rise of Social Theory* (New York: Humanities Press 1963), 360-74.

28 Ibid. (cited), 373.

29 Dooyeweerd, *Roots of Western Culture*, 52.

30 Ibid., 53–4.

31 De Klerk, *Puritans in Africa*, 257.

32 Ibid., 259.

33 Ibid. For a well-documented and moving description of the practical effects of *apartheid* as a political policy in South African society, see Joseph Lelyfeld, *Move Your Shadow: South Africa, Black and White* (New York: Times Books 1985).

34 Nicolaas Diederichs, *Nasionalisme as Lewensbeskouing en sy verhouding tot Internasionalisme* (Nationalism as a view of life and its relationship to Internationalism) (Bloemfontein: Nasionale Pers 1936).

35 Cited in de Klerk, *Puritans in Africa*, 204.

36 Ibid., 206.

37 Cited in Moodie, *Rise of Afrikanerdom*, 47. Moodie points out, however, that, within the Afrikaner spectrum, Malan was a liberal nationalist.

38 Ibid., 161.
39 Ibid., 160.
40 Colin Legum, "Color and Power in the South African Situation," in John Hope Franklin, ed. *Color and Race* (Boston: Houghton Mifflin 1968), 210. Again, however, it is possible that Verwoerd concealed some of the sources of his beliefs from the South African public at large, and that Legum's judgment is incorrect.
41 Cf. Henry Kenney, *Architect of Apartheid: H. F. Verwoerd, an Appraisal* (Johannesburg: Ball 1980), 20.
42 Cf. *Verwoerd Speaks: Speeches, 1948–1966*, ed. A. N. Pelzer (Johannesburg: APB 1966), 208–9.
43 "Day of the Covenant Address at Blood River, December 16, 1958," ibid., 209–20.
44 "Speech on the Occasion of the Opening of the Transkeian Territorial Authority, Umtata, May 7, 1957," ibid., 150–1.
45 Johann-Gottlieb Fichte, *Addresses to the German Nation*, trans. R. F. Jones and G. H. Turnbull, ed. George Armstrong Kelly (New York: Harper and Row 1968), 187–98.
46 Charles Villa-Vicencio, "South Africa's Theologized Nationalism," *Ecumenical Review*, 29, no. 4 (October 1977): 373-82.
47 Kenney, *Architect of Apartheid*, 48–9.
48 See n2 above.
49 De Gruchy, *Church Struggle*, 71.
50 Moodie, *Rise of Afrikanerdom*, 29.
51 Douglas Bax, "The Bible and Apartheid 2," in *Apartheid is a Heresy*, ed. John W. de Gruchy and Charles Villa-Vicencio (Grand Rapids, Mich.: Eerdmans 1983), 142–3.
52 Ibid., 114–17.
53 Ibid., 117.
54 Ibid., 121.
55 Ibid., 122.
56 Ibid., 128.
57 Ibid., 129.
58 Ibid., 131.
59 Ibid., 132.
60 Cited in Peter Walshie, *Church versus State in South Africa: The Case of the Christian Institute* (London: Hurst 1983), 47.

CHAPTER SIX

1 Rodney Carlisle, *The Roots of Black Nationalism* (Port Washington, N.Y.: Kennikat Press 1975), 117.
2 James Deotis Roberts, *Black Theology Today: Liberation and Contextualization* (New York: Mellen Press 1983), 9.

3 Ibid., 59.
4 As, for example, in the writings of James H. Cone: *Black Theology and Black Power* (1969) and *A Black Theology of Liberation* (1970).
5 Carlisle, *Roots of Black Nationalism*, 59.
6 Ibid., 62.
7 C. Eric Lincoln, *The Black Muslims in America* (Boston: Beacon Press 1973), 50.
8 W. E. B. Du Bois, *Darkwater: Voices from the Veil Within* (New York: Harcourt, Brace 1921), 52.
9 Ibid., 245.
10 Gayraud S. Wilmore, in Gayraud S. Wilmore and James H. Cone, eds., *Black Theology: A Documentary History, 1966–1979* (New York: Orbis Books 1979), 243.
11 Ibid.
12 Du Bois, *Darkwater*, 9.
13 Marcus Garvey, "Ethiopia shall once more see the Day of her Glory," in John H. Bracey, Jr., August Meier, and Elliott Rudwick, eds., (Indianapolis: Bobbs-Merrill 1970), 203–4. Garvey's influence, incidentally, extended to South Africa by means of black American mission churches (see Joseph Lelyfeld, *Move Your Shadow: South Africa, Black and White* [New York: Times Books 1985], 223).
14 Eg. A. Philip Randolph, who denounced Garvey as the only negro who could hold rallies in Southern cities and not be lynched because of the affinity between his racial views and those of the Ku Klux Klan. See Bracey, Meier, and Rudwick, *Black Nationalism in America*, 193.
15 Carlisle, *The Roots of Black Nationalism*, 130.
16 W. E. B. Du Bois, "The Conservation of Races," in Howard Brotz, ed., *Negro Social and Political Thought, 1850-1920: Representative Texts* (New York: Basic Books 1966), 484.
17 Ibid., 485.
18 Ibid., 489.
19 Ibid., 488.
20 Ibid., 489.
21 Ibid.
22 W. E. B. Du Bois, "The Revelation of Saint Orgne the Damned," in *W. E. B. Du Bois Speaks: Speeches and Addresses, 1920-1963*, ed. Philip S. Foner (New York: Pathfinder Press 1970), 118.
23 Bishop Henry M. Turner, "God is a Negro," in Bracey, Meier, and Rudwick, eds., *Black Nationalism in America*, 155.
24 Ibid., 154.
25 Du Bois, *Darkwater*, 54.
26 Carlisle, *Roots of Black Nationalism*, 124–5.

27 Albert B. Cleage, Jr., *Black Christian Nationalism: New Directions for the Black Church* (New York: Morrow 1972), xiii.
28 Ibid., xvii.
29 Ibid., xix.
30 Albert B. Cleage, Jr., *The Black Messiah* (New York: Sheed and Ward 1969), 41.
31 Ibid., 99.
32 Ibid., 44; and his *Black Christian Nationalism*, 35.
33 Cleage, *Black Christian Nationalism*, 37.
34 Ibid., 40.
35 Ibid., 251.
36 Ibid., 254.
37 Cleage, *Black Messiah*, 38.
38 Cleage, *Black Christian Nationalism*, 95.
39 According to this myth, the colour black is the progenitor of all that exists – the primal colour; other colours, consequently, are merely shades of black, except for white, which is the absence of black, hence the absence of perfection. All blacks participate in Allah (God) who is the sum of perfection. Since humanity was made in God's image, the first human beings were black: hence, the black Adam. The white race, on the other hand, represents a fall from perfection (i.e., from blackness) which occurred about six thousand years ago when a black scientist named Yakub rebelled against Allah by producing, through a primitive genetic engineering experiment, a new creature with an excess of bad (white) genes. The world thus became populated with "blue-eyed devils" or innately evil beings of inferior mental and physical quality. These evil creatures were allotted by Allah six thousand years of rule (i.e., until almost the present day), after which the lost children of Allah – the oppressed blacks – will be liberated from their bondage. In the final struggle, which will take place in America, the devils will be destroyed and the Nation of Allah will be victorious. See *The End of White World Supremacy: Four Speeches by Malcolm X*, ed. Benjamin Goodman (New York: Merlin House 1971).
40 Cleage, *Black Christian Nationalism*, 101.
41 Ibid., 103.
42 John Mbiti, "An African Views American Black Theology," in Wilmore and Cone, eds., *Black Theology*, 478.
43 James H. Cone, *God of the Oppressed* (New York: Seabury Press 1975), 134.
44 Ibid., 135.
45 James H. Cone, *For My People: Black Theology and the Black Church* (New York: Orbis Books 1984), 66.
46 Cone, *God of the Oppressed*, 136.

47   Cf. James H. Cone, *My Soul Looks Back* (New York: Orbis Books 1986),
     passim.
48   Ibid., 53–6.
49   Rosemary Ruether, "Is There a Black Theology? The Validity and
     Limits of a Racial Perspective," in Rosemary Ruether, ed., *Liberation
     Theology: Human Hope Confronts Christian History and American Power*
     (New York: Paulist Press 1972), 129. Helmut Gollwitzer is wrong when
     he declares that "recent white warnings against black racism and na-
     tionalism obviously ... belong to the chapter of white hypocrisy."
     Helmut Gollwitzer, "Why Black Theology?" in Wilmore and Cone,
     eds., *Black Theology*, 167.

CONCLUSION

1   H. Richard Niebuhr, *Christ and Culture* (New York: Harper 1951), ch. 3.
2   Ibid., 84.
3   Clark M. Williamson, *Has God Rejected His People? Anti-Judaism in the
     Christian Church* (Nashville: Abingdon 1982), 144.
4   Ibid., 145.
5   Karl Barth, "The Jewish Problem and the Christian Answer," *Against
     the Stream: Shorter Post-War Writings, 1946–52* (London: SCM Press
     1954), 199.
6   I cannot find this reference, but, as a former student, I recollect having
     heard Niebuhr say something to this effect in class.
7   Cf. Eulalio R. Baltazar, *The Dark Center: A Process Theology of Blackness*
     (New York: Paulist Press 1973).
8   Joseph R. Washington, Jr., *Anti-Blackness in English Religion, 1500-1800*
     (New York: Edwin Mellen Press 1984).
9   A church whose centre appears to be in Idaho.
10   See Henry de Lesquen et le Club de l'Horloge, *La Politique du vivant*
     (Paris: Albin Michel 1979). This is a neo-racist publication that builds
     much of its case on the findings of the sociobiologists and the students
     of animal behaviour, as well as the psychometricians. Its political flavour
     is strongly authoritarian.
11   Ibid., 29.
12   Francis Galton, *Hereditary Genius* (London: Macmillan 1892).
13   For example, the National Front in Britain. Richard Verrall, its resident
     intellectual, writes as follows: "If sociobiology has buried Marxism,
     what has it given birth to? These latest developments in biology provide
     concrete support for our view of society, which may be termed one
     of 'Social Nationalism'. We believe that in considering the organisation
     of our society it is essential to take into account the biological basis of
     human existence. The nation, first of all, is a 'kin group' in which an

organic social unity (nationalism, as distinct from Marxist class division) is the basis of the group's struggle for existence. Sociobiology has shown us that evolutionary processes have genetically and therefore immutably programmed human nature with instincts of competitiveness, territorial defence, racial prejudice, identification with and integral behaviour within one's kin group (nation), instincts which the Marxist fantasy said were socially determined and which could and should be eradicated." Cited in Martin Barker, *The New Racism: Conservatives and the Ideology of the Tribe* (London: Junction Books 1981), 100. See also Gill Seidel, "Culture, Nation and 'Race' in the British and French New Right," in Ruth Levitas, ed., *The Ideology of the New Right* (Cambridge: Polity Press 1986), 105–35.

14   See the collection edited by Robert Ross entitled *Racism and Colonialism: Essays on Ideology and Social Structure* (The Hague: Nijhoff 1982).

15   Cf. Philip Mason, *Patterns of Dominance* (London: Oxford University Press 1970).

16   David B. Hughes and Evelyn Kallen, *The Anatomy of Racism: Canadian Dimensions* (Montreal: Harvest House 1974), 106.

17   See *World Council of Churches' Statements and Actions on Racism, 1948–1979*, ed. Ans J. van der Bent, Programme to Combat Racism (Geneva: WCC 1980), 30.

18   Hughes and Kallen, *Anatomy of Racism*, 136.

19   Evelyn Kallen, *Ethnicity and Human Rights in Canada* (Toronto: Gage 1982), 132–3. The schools, of course, are inferior because of the supposed inferiority of the aboriginal peoples for whom they are designed.

20   Arthur R. Jensen, "How Much Can We Boost IQ and Scholastic Achievement?" *Harvard Educational Review* 39 (Winter 1969): 1–123, 449–83. Jensen, who became the storm centre of a violent controversy in the United States, wrote as follows: "The [official] belief in the almost infinite plasticity of intellect, the ostrich-like denial of biological factors in individual differences, and the slighting of the role of genetics in the study of intelligence can only hinder investigation and understanding of the conditions, processes and limits through which the social environment influences human behaviour" (ibid., 99).

One forms the impression that Jensen regards himself as a modern Galileo defending scientific truth against obscurantism and persecution. He is no doubt perfectly sincere in his convictions; nevertheless, he told Nixonian America what it wished to hear during the troubled era of the 1960s.

Roughly similar conclusions are drawn by the urban sociologist Edward Banfield in his pessimistic analysis of the (largely black) lower class in America with its restricted time-horizon and its general inability to rise above the social apathy that characterizes its existence. Although

Banfield does not argue on genetic grounds, he does allow for the possibility that the ability to "take account of the future" has something to do with "biologically inherited intelligence" (*The Unheavenly City: The Nature and Future of Our Urban Crisis* [Boston: Little, Brown 1970], 48). As his critics have noted, this analysis represented an academic backlash to the race riots of the 1960s. Like Jensen, Banfield was attacked as a racist by the radical students of the day.

21   Pierre Paraf, *Le Racisme dans le monde* (Paris: Petite Bibliothèque Payot 1981), 69.
22   Barbara Rogers, *Race: No Peace without Justice* (Geneva: World Council of Churches 1980).
23   Sheila D. Collins, *The Economic Basis of Racism and Sexism*, unpublished ms.
24   George Grant, *Technology and Empire: Perspectives on North America* (Toronto: Anansi 1969), 23.
25   Ernest W. Lefever, *Amsterdam to Nairobi: The World Council of Churches and the Third World* (Washington, D.C.: Ethics and Public Policy Center 1979), 41.
26   Ibid., 8.
27   Adam Smith, *The Wealth of Nations* (1776; New York: Modern Library 1937), 599.
28   Vine Deloria, *God Is Red* (New York: Grosset and Dunlap 1973).
29   Reinhold Niebuhr, *The Nature and Destiny of Man*, 2 vols. (New York: Scribner's 1949), 1: 250.

Index

Action Française, 71
Adams, Henry, 146n75
Africa, 6, 80, 90, 107, 109
African Methodist Episcopal Church, 109
African Orthodox Church, 110
Africans, 7, 8, 87
Afrikaans, 96
Afrikaner, Afrikanerdom, 89ff.; antisemitism of, 92; biblical sources for, 97ff.; genius of, 96; German influence within, 95ff.; "holy partiality" in, 95; need for separateness in, 91, 95, 97, 104; opposition to interracial churches, 103, 104; theologized nationalism, 98; whites versus blacks in, 92, 97; Afrikaner Republic, 89, 90
Age of Faith, 17, 21
Age of Imperialism, ix, 80, 122
Age of Reason, 14, 17, 21, 119
Ahlwardt, Hermann, 44
Alexander the Great, 4
Alienation, 57ff.
L'Alliance Israélite universelle, 68
Althaus, Paul, 45, 47, 48, 51, 137n90
Amal, Oscar L., 142n65

America, x, 13, 15, 25, 78, 79, 80ff.; as chosen nation, or race, 83, 84
American Indians, 9, 13
Americas, the, 9
Anglo-Boer War, 90, 148n17
Anglo-Saxons, x, 73ff., 108, 109, 118, 123
Anthropology, 38, 65
Anti-Judaism, 4, 20, 25, 37, 38, 52, 69ff., 74
Antiochus IV Epiphanes, 4
Antisemitism: German racial, 41, 51-2; Medieval, 10; modern, 25, 61ff., 91, 92
Aparthied, xii, 96, 98, 100
Apion of Alexandria, 38
Arendt, Hannah, 129n71, 129n74, 130n88, 143n6
Aristotle, 4, 9, 10, 12
Aryan: as Adamic, 22; Bible, 63; divinity of, 19, 38, 99; features, 24, 61; laws, 50ff., 99; myth, xi, 21ff., 37, 58, 61-4; New Testament, 69; race, 23, 24, 33, 66, 79; religion, 63; as socialist, 64; versus Semite, 61ff.
Aryan Nations, Church of, 121
Asceticism, 7
Auschwitz, 25

Balthazar, Eulalio R., 126n19, 152n7
Baltzell, E. Digby, 146n7
Banfield, Edward, 153n20
Banton, Michael, 143n5
Baptism, 10, 52
Barker, Martin, 128n60, 152n13
Barrés, Maurice, 72
Barth, Karl, 42, 43, 52, 118, 132n8, 136n82, 152n5
Barzun, Jacques, 139n3
Bastide, Roger, 9, 38, 126n18
Bax, Douglas, 100, 102, 149n51
Bellah, Robert, 147n1
Benedict, Ruth, x, 16, 125n4
Berghe, Pierre van den, 24, 132n95
Biddiss, Michael, 18, 57, 58, 129n69
Bismark, Prinie von, 41, 71
Black colour, 5ff.; meaning of, 120
Black Africans, 6ff., 106ff.; symbols of chaos, 92
Black Muslims, 106, 113, 114
Black nation, 105ff.; basis of true Christianity, 110ff.; as God's elect, 111–12; as movement of black liberation, 107; view of white man in, 113